ISBN 9798341317314

Cover design by: Art Painter
Library of Congress Control Number: 2018675309
Printed in the United States of America

CONTENTS

ANDREAOLIVER

Philanthropy Unlocked: How Anyone Can Create Change Through Activism, Volunteering, and Everyday Giving

CONTENTS

ANDREAOLIVER

Philanthropy Unlocked: How Anyone Can Create Change Through Activism, Volunteering, and Everyday Giving

INTRODUCTION: THE POWER OF SMALL ACTS

When most people hear the word *philanthropy*, they imagine wealthy donors writing million-dollar checks or celebrities hosting glamorous charity galas. It's a word that seems reserved for people with deep pockets and powerful connections—the kind of people who can move mountains with a single donation. But here's the thing: *that's a myth.*

Philanthropy, in its truest sense, isn't just about money. It's about caring for the world around you, giving your time, skills, and energy to make it better. Whether you're organizing a local beach cleanup, mentoring a child, or simply advocating for change on social media, *you are a philanthropist.* Every small act of kindness and service contributes to the greater good, and it's these seemingly small actions that can have the most profound effects.

The Myth of Philanthropy: It's More Than Just Giving Money

I once met a woman named Sarah at a community event. She was a single mother, working two jobs just to keep food on the table. "I wish I could do more," she told me. "I don't have money to give, so how can I really help?" Sarah believed she wasn't capable of making a difference because she didn't have financial resources, but as we talked, I could see the passion she had for helping her community. She had been organizing neighborhood events, volunteering at her local shelter, and even created a social media page to advocate for cleaner streets.

Sarah was already doing more than many, but because of the common misconception that philanthropy is only for the rich, she didn't see her own incredible impact. I told her what I'm about to tell you: *you don't need to be rich to be a philanthropist.*

You just need a little bit of passion, creativity, and the belief that your small contributions matter. And they *do* matter—more than you might realize.

Why the World Needs You: Small Acts, Big Change

The world doesn't need another billionaire to save the day. It needs *you.* Right now, where you are, with whatever you have to give. The beauty of change is that it's built on the shoulders of countless small actions, like drops of water that eventually form a powerful river.

Take, for example, the story of Jadav Payeng. He was just one man, living in a remote part of India, who saw his homeland's forests being destroyed by erosion. He wasn't a wealthy tycoon, nor did he have a team of experts to help him, but he started small. Every day, he planted a tree. One tree became ten, ten became hundreds, and decades later, he had single-handedly grown a forest larger than Central Park. *One man, one small action—an incredible, lasting impact.*

The lesson here is simple: you don't have to do it all at once, and you certainly don't have to do it alone. But you can start today, and what you do matters more than you know.

The Ripple Effect: How Small Gestures Reach Far Beyond Their Origin

The idea of the ripple effect is one of my favorite metaphors for how change happens. You drop a pebble into a pond, and the ripples move outward, expanding far beyond the initial point of impact. That's what happens when you take small actions in service of others—they spread, touching lives you may never meet, in ways you may never see.

Let me tell you about a group of high school students in a small town who decided to tackle food insecurity. They didn't have money to donate, but they had a lot of enthusiasm and a few extra hours after school. They started a simple project: collecting leftover food from the cafeteria and delivering it to a local shelter. Soon, the school administration got involved, local businesses donated supplies, and volunteers from the community joined the effort. What started as a small, local act of kindness evolved into a community-wide initiative, providing hundreds of meals a month to those in need.

The ripple effect of those students' actions went far beyond their original intention. Not only did they feed people, but they also inspired others to get involved, showing that anyone, anywhere, can spark change. Your actions, no matter how small, can create ripples too.

You Already Have What It Takes: Passion, Creativity, and Commitment

Here's the best part: *you already have what it takes to make a difference.* You don't need wealth, celebrity, or powerful connections. You just need to tap into your passion, think outside the box, and commit to taking action—even if it's just a small one.

Look around you. What are you passionate about? Is it protecting the environment, helping people in your local community, or advocating for human rights? Maybe you love working with children or have a knack for organizing events. Whatever your passion, there's a way for you to channel it into meaningful impact.

Consider these out-of-the-box ideas:

- Are you a great cook? Host a community dinner where the proceeds go to a cause you care about.
- Love hiking? Start a group that cleans up local trails and promotes conservation.
- Enjoy painting? Use your art to raise awareness about climate change or donate pieces to charity auctions.
- Good at social media? Become a digital activist, using your platforms to spread awareness about humanitarian issues or environmental sustainability.

You already have the tools—your unique skills, passions, and ideas—now it's just about putting them to work. The opportunities are endless, and with a bit of creativity, you can make an impact in ways you may never have imagined.

You Are Needed, Now More Than Ever

The world is full of challenges, from environmental destruction to humanitarian crises. It's easy to feel overwhelmed by the scale of the problems we face. But here's the truth: *you don't need to fix everything to make a difference*. You just need to start.

Remember Sarah? She thought she wasn't doing enough, but she was already changing her community in small but meaningful ways. Just like her, you have the power to create change, and the world needs people like you to step up. Not tomorrow, not when you have more time or resources, but right now.

So, as you read this book, keep one thing in mind: *every small act matters*. And the beautiful thing is, those small acts add up. Together, we can create a ripple effect that changes the world, one small action at a time.

Now, let's get started.

PART I: FINDING YOUR CAUSE

CHAPTER 1: START WITH WHAT MATTERS TO YOU

When it comes to getting involved in philanthropy, the first step isn't about the *how*—it's about the *why*. What drives you? What wakes you up in the morning with a sense of urgency? What issue can you not stop thinking about when you see it on the news or hear about it in your community?

I'm sure you've heard the old saying, "Do what you love, and you'll never work a day in your life." The same idea applies to philanthropy. The more you care about the cause, the more motivated you'll be to get involved and stay involved. Philanthropy is deeply personal, and the best way to start is by reflecting on what truly matters to you.

Reflecting on Your Values: How to Discover Which Causes Ignite Your Passion

I want to introduce you to a man named James. James spent his whole life in the corporate world, climbing the ladder, earning promotions, and enjoying all the perks that came with it. But despite his professional success, he felt an emptiness. He knew he wanted to give back, but with so many issues facing the world —hunger, poverty, environmental degradation—he didn't know where to start.

One day, while driving to work, he saw a patch of forest being cleared to make way for a new shopping mall. It broke his heart. As a child, he had spent countless hours exploring the woods behind his house, learning about the environment and developing a deep appreciation for nature. That's when it hit him: he cared deeply about the environment. Protecting it wasn't just an idea—it was a *core value* of his. From that moment on, he decided to dedicate his time to environmental causes. He started small, joining a local conservation group. Now, he leads a campaign to protect green spaces in his community.

James found his cause by reconnecting with a core value he had as a child, and it was that connection that gave him the passion to dive into his philanthropy work.

So, how do *you* discover your cause? It starts with reflection. Take some time to think about the issues that move you emotionally. Ask yourself:

- **What makes me angry or sad when I hear about it?** Is it homelessness in your city? The state of the oceans? The plight of refugees around the world?
- **What brings me joy when I contribute to it?** Think about the last time you felt genuinely excited to help someone. Was it teaching a child? Helping a neighbor with groceries? Planting a tree?
- **What values do I hold dear?** Is it justice, equality, sustainability, compassion? Your values are often the key to unlocking your passion for a particular cause.
- **What personal experiences have shaped my views?** Many people find their cause through their life experiences. If you or someone close to you has struggled with an illness, you might feel drawn to supporting healthcare initiatives. If you grew up in a community that lacked resources, you might want to give back to underserved neighborhoods.

Once you have some clarity on what matters to you, you're ready to start exploring the causes that align with your values. This isn't a rushed process. Take your time and allow yourself to feel the pull toward a cause that resonates deeply.

Environmental vs. Humanitarian Causes: Understanding the Differences and Similarities

When you think about causes, it often helps to divide them into broad categories. For many people, the choice comes down to environmental or humanitarian causes. Let's explore both to help you decide where your heart might lie.

Environmental Causes: Protecting the Planet

Environmental causes focus on the natural world—protecting ecosystems, fighting climate change, preserving biodiversity, and promoting sustainable living. These causes are often driven by a desire to protect the planet for future generations and ensure that the natural beauty and resources we enjoy today will be available tomorrow.

When it comes to environmental philanthropy, there are so many areas where you can make an impact. For example:

- **Conservation and Wildlife Protection**: Think of groups like the World Wildlife Fund or local organizations that protect endangered species or restore habitats.
- **Climate Action**: This might involve supporting renewable energy initiatives, advocating for policy changes, or working to reduce carbon emissions.
- **Sustainable Living**: You could focus on promoting recycling, reducing waste, or educating people about sustainable agriculture practices.
- **Pollution Reduction**: Efforts to reduce plastic pollution in oceans or clean up air and water quality are critical to a healthy planet.

If you've ever felt moved when watching a documentary about deforestation, the melting ice caps, or the devastation caused by pollution, environmental philanthropy could be the right path for you.

One of my favorite examples of grassroots environmental activism comes from a small group of friends in the UK who started a community recycling initiative. They noticed their town had no formal recycling program, so they took matters into their own hands. They set up collection points in local shops and encouraged their neighbors to recycle plastic, paper, and glass. Soon, their efforts attracted media attention, and the local government partnered with them to develop a formal recycling plan for the town. Their passion for the environment turned a small action into widespread change.

Humanitarian Causes: Helping People in Need

Humanitarian causes focus on the well-being of people—whether it's alleviating poverty, supporting healthcare, promoting human rights, or providing disaster relief. These causes often aim to improve the quality of life for individuals and communities, particularly those who are marginalized or in crisis.

Some areas of humanitarian philanthropy include:

- **Poverty Alleviation**: Supporting efforts to provide food, shelter, and economic opportunities to people living in poverty.
- **Healthcare Access**: Volunteering or donating to organizations that provide medical care to underserved populations.
- **Education**: Working to improve access to quality education, particularly in underprivileged areas.
- **Human Rights Advocacy**: Supporting the fight for equality, justice, and freedom for all individuals, regardless of race, gender, or nationality.

- **Refugee and Disaster Relief**: Providing support to people affected by natural disasters or conflict, often through organizations like the Red Cross or Doctors Without Borders.

If you're someone who feels a strong desire to help people—whether it's a neighbor in need or a community across the globe—humanitarian causes might resonate most with you. These causes often appeal to people with a deep sense of empathy and a desire to ensure that everyone has access to basic human needs.

One incredible story that highlights the power of humanitarian action comes from a young woman named Malala Yousafzai. At a very young age, Malala became an advocate for girls' education in Pakistan, where the Taliban had banned girls from attending school. Her passion for education and equality led her to speak out against the oppression she witnessed in her own community. Despite facing threats and even surviving an assassination attempt, Malala continued her activism. Today, she's a global symbol of courage, and her foundation has helped millions of girls access education. Her story shows that one person, driven by a humanitarian cause, can change the world.

Local vs. Global Impact: Deciding Where You Want to Make a Difference

Once you've figured out the cause that speaks to you, the next question is: *Where do you want to make your impact?* Do you want to focus your efforts in your own backyard, or are you passionate about tackling issues on a global scale? There's no right or wrong answer—it's about what feels meaningful to you.

Local Impact: Starting at Home

Sometimes, the most rewarding and effective way to make a difference is to start right where you are. Local impact allows you to directly see the changes you're making in your own community, and the connection you'll have with the people and issues you're helping can be incredibly powerful.

Here are some examples of how you can get involved locally:

- **Volunteer at a Local Nonprofit**: Whether it's a food bank, animal shelter, or environmental organization, there are always local nonprofits that need a helping hand.
- **Support Community Development Projects**: You could join efforts to improve local parks, build affordable housing, or provide after-school programs for kids.
- **Organize Local Events**: Host a fundraising event, educational workshop, or neighborhood clean-up to bring attention to a cause you care about.
- **Advocate for Change at the Local Level**: You can work with local government officials to implement policies that align with your cause, whether it's environmental protection or improving social services.

Take the example of Rebecca, who lives in a small town that was struggling with a lack of affordable housing. Rather than waiting for someone else to solve the problem, Rebecca rallied her community to start a volunteer-run project building tiny homes for those in need. The impact was immediate: families who had been living in cars or couch-surfing suddenly had safe, stable housing. And because it was a local effort, the project quickly gained support from neighbors, local businesses, and even the town council.

If you want to see the direct effects of your efforts and build stronger connections with the people around you, focusing on local causes is an amazing way to give back.

Global Impact: Reaching Beyond Borders

On the other hand, maybe your heart is pulled toward global issues—poverty in developing nations, access to clean water, the plight of refugees, or large-scale environmental challenges like deforestation or climate change. Global impact can be incredibly fulfilling because you know you're contributing to solutions for some of the world's most urgent problems.

Here are some ways you can make a global impact:

- **Support International Nonprofits**: Organizations like Oxfam, UNICEF, and the World Wildlife Fund work across the globe to address pressing humanitarian and environmental issues.
- **Participate in International Volunteering Programs**: Some people choose to spend a few weeks or months volunteering abroad, helping with everything from building schools to teaching English or supporting healthcare initiatives.
- **Advocate for Global Change from Home**: Even if you can't travel, you can still support global causes by raising awareness online, participating in global campaigns, or writing to your government representatives about international policy issues.
- **Donate to Global Crowdfunding Campaigns**: Sites like GoFundMe and GlobalGiving allow you to support grassroots projects around the world, often with as little as a few dollars.

Take the story of Greta Thunberg, a teenager who became the face of the global climate movement. Greta's activism began with her protesting alone outside the Swedish parliament. But her passion and commitment to addressing climate change quickly spread, inspiring millions of people around the world to join the fight. Her message crossed borders, and today she's one of the most influential voices in environmental advocacy. Greta's story shows that global impact doesn't always mean traveling far—it can start right where you are and ripple out across the world.

You Don't Have to Choose Right Away

Whether you decide to focus on environmental or humanitarian causes, and whether you start at home or aim for global impact, the important thing is to take that first step. You don't have to know everything or have all the answers before you start. What matters is that you *start*.

Take the time to reflect on your values, passions, and skills. Ask yourself what brings you joy, what makes you angry, and what moves you to take action. Whether you're inspired by the beauty of nature or the need to help those who are struggling, there's a cause out there that needs your unique contribution.

And remember, you don't have to do this alone. The world is full of people just like you—people who care, people who are ready to make a difference. Together, we can create change, one small act at a time.

In the next chapter, we'll explore the various ways you can get involved—whether you're ready to dive into activism, offer your skills as a volunteer, or start your own community project. No matter what resources you have, there's a way for you to start making an impact today.

CHAPTER 2: ALIGNING YOUR SKILLS AND TALENTS

When we think about philanthropy, we often picture it as something that requires giving time, money, or physical effort—maybe volunteering at a shelter, donating to a charity, or joining a community clean-up. While these are all valuable contributions, there's another way to get involved that can be even more powerful: using the skills and talents you already have.

Imagine you're an artist, accountant, teacher, or coder. Maybe you run a small business, or you're a master gardener in your spare time. Whatever your unique strengths may be, those talents can be incredibly useful to nonprofits and causes that need specialized help. The key to making a real difference is aligning your skills with the causes that need them.

Let's break this down, starting with a simple question: **What do you bring to the table?**

What Do You Bring to the Table?: Identifying Your Unique Skills and Strengths

Every one of us has unique talents and skills that can be used to help others. Whether you're a numbers person, a creative thinker, a tech guru, or just really good at organizing things, you have something valuable to offer. The first step is identifying those strengths and figuring out how they can align with the causes you care about.

Let me tell you about Maria. Maria is a graphic designer who, for years, felt a bit disconnected from the idea of philanthropy. She wasn't in a position to donate large sums of money, and she didn't think her skills were relevant to the humanitarian and environmental causes she cared about. One day, a friend asked if she could help design a flyer for a local charity event. That small task led to a lightbulb moment—Maria realized her design skills could make a massive impact by helping nonprofits spread their message, attract donors, and organize events. Soon, Maria was using her talents to support several organizations, and she found a renewed sense of purpose in her work.

Maria's story shows that you don't need to overhaul your life to get involved in philanthropy. Sometimes, it's as simple as using what you already know how to do and applying it in a new way.

How to Identify Your Skills

To get started, think about what you're naturally good at or what you've learned through your job, hobbies, or education. Ask yourself these questions:

- **What do I enjoy doing?** Is it writing, organizing, teaching, problem-solving? Your enjoyment is a clue to where your talents lie.
- **What am I skilled at?** Consider your professional abilities (e.g., marketing, finance, tech, healthcare) as well as personal skills like communication, creativity, or leadership.
- **What do people often ask me for help with?** If friends, family, or colleagues turn to you for advice on specific topics, it's a sign that you've got valuable expertise in that area.

- **What would I do for free, just because I love it?** The things you're willing to do for fun or as a hobby often align with your passions and skills.

If you're struggling to identify your talents, ask those around you for feedback. Sometimes, others see our strengths more clearly than we do. Once you have a sense of what you bring to the table, it's time to consider how those skills can be put to work in the world of philanthropy.

Leveraging What You Have: How Your Professional Skills Can Be Invaluable to Nonprofit Causes

It's one thing to have skills; it's another to realize how those skills can change the world. Let's look at a few common professional abilities and how they can be leveraged to make a meaningful impact.

1. Marketing and Communication

Are you a marketer or content creator? Nonprofits often struggle to get their message out to the public, attract donors, and build awareness for their causes. If you have experience in social media, branding, or public relations, your expertise can be a game-changer.

Take the example of Julie, a digital marketing specialist who started volunteering her time at a small animal rescue organization. The rescue had a shoestring budget and very little online presence. Julie helped them set up a simple social media strategy, created engaging content, and ran targeted ads on Facebook. Within a few months, the organization saw an increase in donations, volunteer sign-ups, and pet adoptions. By using her marketing skills, Julie amplified the organization's reach in ways they couldn't have achieved on their own.

If you have experience in marketing, consider helping a nonprofit revamp their website, run an ad campaign, or create a cohesive social media presence. These efforts can drive real results and make a lasting impact.

2. Graphic Design and Visual Arts

As we saw in Maria's story, graphic design can be an incredibly powerful tool in the nonprofit world. From creating flyers and brochures to designing websites or social media graphics, visual storytelling is essential for engaging supporters and spreading awareness.

Take Andy, a freelance graphic designer, who partnered with a conservation organization to design an interactive, visually stunning annual report. By transforming dry statistics into engaging infographics and compelling visuals, Andy helped the organization communicate their impact in a way that inspired new donors and secured additional funding.

If you're a designer, photographer, or visual artist, there are countless opportunities to support causes that need eye-catching visuals. Your work can be the difference between an organization's message getting noticed or getting lost in the noise.

3. Technology and Web Development

In today's digital age, every organization needs a solid online presence, but many nonprofits lack the resources to build or maintain a functional website. If you're skilled in web development, coding, or IT, your abilities are in high demand.

Consider Dan, a web developer who volunteered with a nonprofit that provides clean water to communities in developing countries. The organization's outdated website made it difficult for them to receive donations or communicate their impact. Dan stepped in and created a user-friendly site that not only boosted their online donations but also made it easier for potential volunteers and supporters to get involved. That small contribution made a big difference in the nonprofit's ability to operate effectively.

If you have tech skills, you can offer to build or update a nonprofit's website, develop apps or online tools that support their mission, or simply provide technical support to help them run more smoothly.

4. Finance and Accounting

Nonprofits often face the challenge of managing their finances effectively, particularly when they have limited resources and staff. If you're an accountant, financial planner, or have experience in bookkeeping, your expertise can be invaluable to organizations that need help with budgeting, financial reporting, and tax compliance.

Consider Liza, an accountant who volunteered with a local homeless shelter. The shelter was struggling to keep track of donations, manage expenses, and prepare their financial reports for grant applications. Liza stepped in to organize their finances, develop a clear budget, and help them apply for grants. Her efforts helped the shelter secure more funding, allowing them to expand their services and support more people in need.

If you have financial expertise, offering to help a nonprofit with their books, create financial plans, or apply for grants can make a significant impact on their sustainability and growth.

5. Healthcare and Social Work

If you work in healthcare, counseling, or social services, there are countless ways to make an impact by offering your expertise to underserved populations. Medical professionals, nurses, therapists, and social workers are often needed in communities that lack access to adequate healthcare or support services.

One inspiring example is Dr. Anthony, a pediatrician who started volunteering at a free clinic in his city's underserved neighborhoods. The clinic relied on volunteer medical professionals to provide care for families who couldn't afford regular healthcare. Dr. Anthony's weekly contributions—just a few hours of his time—helped improve the health outcomes of hundreds of children. It wasn't about grand gestures; it was about showing up regularly, using his skills to make a difference where it was needed most.

If you have a background in healthcare or social work, you can volunteer at clinics, provide counseling or support to those in need, or help run health education programs in your community or abroad.

Personal Passions in Action: Finding Ways to Integrate What You Love into the Causes You Care About

Beyond professional skills, your personal passions—whether it's gardening, music, or even knitting—can also be used to support the causes you care about. The key is finding creative ways to combine what you love doing with the needs of the community or nonprofit organizations around you.

1. Gardening and the Environment

If you love spending time in the garden, why not use that passion to support environmental causes? Take Sophie, an avid gardener who started a community garden in an urban area with little access to fresh produce. What started as a small project to beautify her neighborhood quickly became a food source for local families, a learning space for children, and a way to promote sustainable agriculture. Sophie was able to turn her personal love of gardening into a community asset that made a tangible difference in people's lives.

You could start a similar initiative—whether it's planting trees, creating pollinator-friendly spaces, or organizing community composting programs. Your passion for gardening can become a tool for environmental education and food sustainability.

2. Coding and Tech for Good

Let's talk about Ayesha, a software developer who loved building apps in her free time. After hearing about the refugee crisis in Europe, Ayesha wanted to help but wasn't sure how. She decided to create an app that connected refugees with essential services like housing, legal aid, and healthcare. The app became a crucial resource for thousands of displaced people, offering them a lifeline in difficult times. Ayesha's passion for coding became a direct way to help people in need.

If you're passionate about technology, there are endless possibilities to use those skills for social good. Whether it's developing educational apps, building platforms to connect volunteers, or creating tools to monitor environmental impact, tech is a powerful way to make a difference.

3. Music, Art, and Cultural Expression

For those with creative talents, the arts offer a unique way to engage with causes. Music, art, and cultural expression can be used to raise awareness, inspire change, and bring people together.

Consider the story of Luis, a musician who organized a series of benefit concerts to raise money for disaster relief after a hurricane devastated a coastal town. The concerts not only raised funds but also brought the community together, reminding people of their shared humanity in times of crisis. Luis used his passion for music as a platform for both fundraising and healing.

If you're an artist, musician, or performer, you can organize events that benefit your chosen cause, donate your work to charity auctions, or use your platform to raise awareness about important issues.

You Already Have What It Takes

The beauty of aligning your skills and passions with philanthropy is that it allows you to give in a way that feels natural and fulfilling. You don't need to reinvent yourself or take on roles that feel foreign to you. By simply offering what you already know how to do, you can make a profound impact.

Whether you're a graphic designer, an accountant, a coder, or a gardener, there's a place for your talents in the world of philanthropy. The key is to recognize that what you bring to the table is valuable, and that by leveraging your skills in creative ways, you can help change lives, improve communities, and make the world a better place.

So, what do you bring to the table? Think about your unique skills and passions, and start looking for opportunities to put them to use. You already have what it takes to make a difference—all you need to do is take that first step.

PART II: WAYS TO GET INVOLVED—NO MONEY REQUIRED

CHAPTER 3: THE POWER OF ACTIVISM

You don't need money to change the world. You don't need to be a CEO or a billionaire philanthropist to make an impact. What you do need is passion, commitment, and a belief that your voice—yes, your voice—can influence real change. At its core, activism is about speaking up, standing up, and pushing for a better, more just world. And the beauty of activism is that anyone, anywhere, can participate, often with little more than time and creativity.

Why Activism Matters: The Role of Advocacy in Changing Systems

Throughout history, activism has been the driving force behind some of the most significant social, environmental, and political changes. From the Civil Rights Movement to the fight for women's suffrage to the global environmental movements of today, it has always been ordinary people who decided to stand up and demand something better. These were not people with limitless resources, but people who believed in the power of advocacy and collective action to change systems.

Think about Rosa Parks. Her refusal to give up her bus seat in 1955 wasn't a grand financial gesture, but a powerful act of resistance that helped spark the Montgomery Bus Boycott. It was a simple action, but one rooted in deep conviction, and it played a pivotal role in the larger Civil Rights Movement. That's the thing about activism: sometimes, it's the smallest actions that create the biggest ripples.

Activism matters because it challenges the status quo. It shines a light on injustice, forces conversations that might otherwise be silenced, and holds those in power accountable. Whether you're advocating for environmental justice, human rights, or systemic reform, activism is a way to make your voice heard and push for change, even when it seems like the odds are against you.

And here's the best part: activism is free. You don't need to write a big check to an organization. You don't need to have wealth or connections. You just need the will to act—and that can look a hundred different ways.

Creative Activism: How Art, Storytelling, and Social Media Can Spread Awareness and Drive Action

Activism is not one-size-fits-all. You don't have to be marching in the streets to be an activist, although that's certainly one powerful form of advocacy. In today's world, activism is getting more creative, more adaptable, and more accessible, and it can be shaped by your unique talents and passions.

The Power of Art in Activism

Take art, for example. Art has always been a tool for activism, used to challenge societal norms, provoke thought, and inspire change. Think of the powerful street art that covered the walls of Berlin as the wall was falling, or the way political cartoons have shaped public opinion for centuries. Art speaks to people in ways that words sometimes cannot. It has the ability to evoke emotions, stir conversation, and galvanize communities around a cause.

A recent example of creative activism is the work of French artist JR, who has created large-scale art installations around the world to bring attention to social issues. One of his most striking projects was a giant portrait of a Mexican child, pasted on the border fence between the U.S. and Mexico. The image, titled *Kikito*, portrayed the child peeking over the fence, looking curiously into the U.S. It was a silent but powerful statement on immigration and border politics—no words needed, just an image that spoke volumes.

If you have a creative talent, whether it's painting, writing, photography, or filmmaking, you can use it to amplify a cause. Maybe you design a series of posters promoting climate action and hang them in your neighborhood. Maybe you create a short documentary about food insecurity in your community. Maybe you write poetry that speaks to the struggles of refugees and share it online. Whatever your medium, art is a way to reach people's hearts and minds in a way that facts and figures often can't.

Storytelling as Activism

Beyond visual art, storytelling itself is a form of activism. Personal stories have a way of connecting with people on a deeper level, humanizing issues that can otherwise feel distant or abstract. Think about Malala Yousafzai. Her personal story of being shot by the Taliban for advocating for girls' education didn't just draw attention to her individual courage; it highlighted a global issue—the lack of access to education for girls around the world. Malala's story moved millions and turned her into an international advocate for education.

You don't need to have a story as dramatic as Malala's to be an activist storyteller. Sometimes, the simple act of sharing your own experiences or those of others can spark change. If you're passionate about environmental justice, for example, you might share the story of a local community impacted by pollution or climate change. If you care about mental health, you might write a blog post about your own struggles and advocate for better access to mental health services.

Everyone has a story, and those stories have power. So, share them. Use social media, blogs, podcasts, or local events to tell your story and encourage others to do the same. Storytelling helps us see beyond the statistics and policies—it reminds us that behind every issue are real people whose lives are being affected.

Social Media: A Megaphone for Activism

In today's digital age, social media has become one of the most powerful tools for activism. It's essentially a megaphone that allows individuals to amplify their voices, reach larger audiences, and mobilize communities for action. And the best part? It's accessible to anyone with an internet connection.

Consider the #BlackLivesMatter movement. What started as a hashtag following the 2013 acquittal of Trayvon Martin's killer became a global movement against racial injustice. Through social media, the movement gained momentum, organized protests, and brought attention to systemic racism and police brutality in ways traditional media often didn't. Social media gave people a platform to share their stories, spread information, and organize in real time.

Another powerful example is the climate activism of Greta Thunberg. Greta began her climate strikes alone in front of the Swedish parliament, but through social media, her message spread worldwide. Soon, millions of young people were joining her in climate strikes, organizing protests, and demanding action from governments.

You don't need a massive following to make an impact on social media. Here's how you can get started with digital activism:

- **Share Information**: Whether it's posting about an issue you care about or sharing educational content from reputable sources, you can use your platform to inform others.
- **Amplify Voices**: Retweet, repost, or share stories from activists, organizations, or communities whose voices might otherwise go unheard.
- **Call to Action**: Use social media to encourage your followers to take specific actions—sign a petition, attend

a protest, or support a cause.

- **Join Movements**: Use hashtags to connect with global movements like #FridaysForFuture (climate action), #MeToo (gender equality), or #RefugeesWelcome (support for refugees).

Digital activism allows you to engage with people across the world, raising awareness and inspiring action without ever leaving your home.

Digital Advocacy: Starting Petitions, Online Campaigns, and Using Your Voice on Social Media Platforms

Let's dive deeper into digital advocacy and how you can use the internet to create real-world change. One of the most effective tools at your disposal is the online petition. In just a few minutes, you can start a petition that brings attention to an issue you care about and encourages others to join you in demanding change.

Starting a Petition

Take Avaaz.org, for example. Avaaz is a global online activism platform where users can create petitions on everything from climate action to human rights. One successful petition launched by Avaaz was aimed at banning bee-killing pesticides in Europe. The petition garnered over 2 million signatures and helped influence policymakers to pass a ban on those harmful pesticides. That's the power of collective action through digital tools.

If you feel strongly about an issue—whether it's stopping deforestation, improving access to mental health services, or pushing for local environmental policies—you can start a petition and share it with your community. Here's how to get started:

1. **Choose a Platform**: There are several online platforms where you can create petitions, including Change.org, Avaaz, and Care2.
2. **Be Specific**: The most successful petitions are clear and

actionable. Don't just call for broad change; focus on specific, measurable outcomes. For example, instead of "Protect the Environment," your petition might be "Ban Single-Use Plastics in Our City."

3. **Tell a Story**: Personal stories resonate with people more than just facts. Explain why this issue matters to you and how it affects real people or the environment.
4. **Promote It**: Once your petition is live, share it widely —on social media, via email, and with local groups. Ask others to share it as well, and watch your message spread.

Creating Online Campaigns

Beyond petitions, you can also create full-blown online campaigns to rally support around a cause. Think about the Ice Bucket Challenge, which went viral in 2014 to raise awareness for ALS (amyotrophic lateral sclerosis). People around the world participated, dumping ice water over their heads, sharing videos on social media, and donating to ALS research. The campaign raised over $115 million for ALS research and showed how online challenges can turn awareness into action.

You can get creative with online campaigns, whether it's starting a hashtag challenge, organizing a virtual event, or creating shareable content like infographics or videos. The key is to engage people in a way that's fun, interactive, and easy to share.

Hosting "House" Events: Bringing People Together to Educate, Motivate, and Brainstorm Collective Actions

While digital activism is powerful, sometimes the most meaningful impact comes from gathering people together in person. Hosting events in your home—or even virtually—can be a fantastic way to educate, motivate, and inspire collective action.

What Is a "House" Event?

A "house" event is essentially a small gathering of people united by a common cause. These events can be informal and intimate, making them the perfect setting for discussions, brainstorming sessions, and community-building. Whether you're hosting in your living room, at a local coffee shop, or online, house events are about fostering meaningful connections and turning those connections into action.

Why House Events Matter

Think about it: some of the most powerful movements in history started with small groups of people coming together in living rooms, church basements, or community centers. The Civil Rights Movement, for example, relied heavily on house meetings to organize and strategize. These small gatherings became the foundation for larger-scale protests, marches, and policy changes.

Hosting a house event allows you to create a space for education and action, where people can learn about an issue, share ideas, and figure out tangible steps they can take together.

How to Host a House Event

1. **Choose a Focus**: What issue are you passionate about? Is it climate change, refugee rights, or access to clean water? Your event should have a clear focus so participants know what to expect.
2. **Invite the Right People**: Start with your friends, family, and local community. You don't need a large group—sometimes a handful of passionate people can make the biggest difference.
3. **Educate and Inspire**: At the event, provide information on the issue. You might show a short documentary, invite a guest speaker, or lead a discussion about why the cause matters.
4. **Brainstorm Action Steps**: After the education portion, shift to action. What can you all do together to support this cause? Could you start a local campaign, organize a fundraiser, or volunteer as a group?

5. **Stay Connected**: After the event, keep the momentum going by creating a group chat, email list, or social media page where everyone can stay updated on future actions.

Activism Is for Everyone

You don't need deep pockets to be an activist. You don't even need to be an expert on the issues. What you need is the courage to stand up, speak out, and take action in whatever way makes sense for you. Whether you're painting murals, writing stories, organizing petitions, or gathering friends in your living room, your voice has power.

Activism isn't just about the big, headline-making moments—it's about the small, everyday actions that build momentum and create lasting change. And the best part? You can start today, no money required. So go ahead—use your creativity, your skills, and your voice to make the world a better place. The power of activism is in your hands.

CHAPTER 4: VOLUNTEERING YOUR TIME

The most valuable thing you can give to a cause isn't necessarily money—it's your time. In a world where many nonprofits, grassroots organizations, and community initiatives are stretched thin, the simple act of volunteering can make an extraordinary difference. Volunteering your time is one of the most powerful and accessible ways to create real change, no matter your background, your skillset, or your resources. And the best part? It's something anyone can do.

How Time Equals Change: The Importance of Volunteering for Causes That Need People Power

We often hear the phrase "time is money," and while there's some truth to that, time can be even more valuable when it's offered freely in service of others. Nonprofits and charities run on what I like to call "people power"—the energy, effort, and commitment of volunteers who help keep their programs running and their services accessible.

Take, for example, a local animal shelter. Many such shelters rely almost entirely on volunteers to walk dogs, clean cages, organize adoption events, and handle administrative tasks. Without this army of dedicated individuals, most shelters simply couldn't function. It's not glamorous work, but it's essential. For every hour a volunteer spends walking a dog or comforting a nervous cat, they're not just caring for an animal—they're giving that animal a better chance at finding a forever home.

Or consider a food bank. Many food banks depend heavily on volunteers to sort donations, pack boxes, and distribute food to families in need. In these organizations, time truly equals change. Each volunteer hour translates into meals for hungry families, comfort for those who are struggling, and a sense of security in the community.

And this doesn't just apply to animal shelters and food banks —volunteering touches almost every sector of society. Whether you're working on environmental conservation, human rights, education, or healthcare, the time you give plays a critical role in driving change forward.

Volunteering in Action: The Story of Theresa

Theresa, a full-time accountant and mother of two, had always wanted to give back to her community but didn't feel like she had the time. Between her job, her kids' schedules, and the general busyness of life, volunteering seemed impossible. Then one summer, she noticed an article in her local paper about a literacy program for at-risk youth. The program was desperately seeking volunteers to help tutor children who were struggling to read. Something clicked for Theresa—she'd always loved reading and knew how important literacy was for future success.

So, she decided to volunteer. Despite her packed schedule, Theresa carved out just two hours every week to tutor at her local library. The impact was immediate. One of the children she worked with, a quiet boy named Michael, started improving rapidly. After a few weeks, he began reading out loud with confidence, and soon he was picking out books on his own to take home. By the end of the summer, his reading scores had jumped, and his teachers reported a noticeable change in his attitude toward school.

For Theresa, those two hours a week didn't feel like much, but for Michael, it was life-changing. That's the thing about volunteering your time: you might never know the full impact of your efforts, but for those you help, it could be profound.

Virtual Volunteering: Opportunities to Make an Impact from Your Home

In today's digital age, volunteering isn't limited to physically showing up somewhere. Virtual volunteering has opened up an entirely new realm of opportunities for people to give back from the comfort of their own homes. Whether you're tutoring a student halfway across the world, providing professional advice to a nonprofit, or helping spread awareness on social media, virtual volunteering allows you to make a difference no matter where you are.

Virtual Tutoring and Mentoring

One of the most popular forms of virtual volunteering is tutoring or mentoring. Many organizations are seeking volunteers to help students with their schoolwork, especially in underserved areas where access to quality education is limited.

Take the example of David, a retired teacher who wanted to continue helping students but was no longer able to commute to schools. He discovered a virtual tutoring program where he could help students from different parts of the country with reading and math through video calls. David was matched with a high school student named Maria, who was struggling with algebra. They met twice a week online, and over the course of several months, Maria's grades improved, and her confidence in math grew. Even though David never met Maria in person, his virtual support made a huge difference in her academic journey.

Programs like this exist all over the world, and the beauty of virtual tutoring is that you can do it from anywhere, fitting it into your schedule at times that work best for you.

Consulting for Nonprofits

If you have specialized skills in areas like marketing, finance, web development, or law, your expertise can be invaluable to nonprofits, and much of this work can be done virtually. Many small nonprofits and grassroots organizations lack the budget to hire professionals, which means they rely on volunteers to help with everything from creating websites to drafting business plans.

For example, Emily, a graphic designer, started volunteering her time by creating social media graphics and promotional materials for a nonprofit that worked with refugees. She spent a few hours each month designing posters, brochures, and infographics, all from her home office. Her work helped the organization increase their visibility and reach more donors, all without Emily ever stepping foot in their office.

Virtual consulting allows you to use your professional skills for good, offering nonprofits the expertise they need to grow and succeed, often with just a few hours of your time each month.

Social Media Volunteering

Social media is a powerful tool for change, and if you're savvy with platforms like Instagram, Twitter, or Facebook, you can use your skills to help nonprofits spread their message, raise awareness, and mobilize support. Many organizations, especially smaller ones, need help managing their social media accounts, creating content, and engaging with their online communities.

A great example of this is Chloe, a college student who volunteered to manage the Instagram account for a local environmental group. Chloe was passionate about climate action and wanted to help, but didn't have much time to commit in person. Instead, she offered to help boost their online presence. She created engaging posts, shared stories about local environmental issues, and encouraged followers to attend events. Over the course of a few months, the organization's online following grew, leading to more participation in clean-up events and greater awareness of environmental challenges in the area.

If you're comfortable with social media, this is a fantastic way to make an impact without ever leaving your home.

Local Community Service: Finding Volunteer Opportunities in Your Neighborhood

While virtual volunteering is a great option, there's something uniquely rewarding about getting involved in your own community. Local community service allows you to see the direct impact of your work, build connections with people around you, and strengthen the place you call home.

Beach Clean-Ups and Environmental Projects

One of the most popular forms of local volunteering is participating in environmental projects like beach clean-ups, tree planting, or park restoration. These efforts not only improve the local environment but also bring communities together around a common cause.

Take Jacob, for example. After moving to a coastal town, he noticed that the local beaches were often littered with trash after busy weekends. Rather than just complain, Jacob decided to take action. He organized a small beach clean-up with a few friends, and over time, the group grew into a regular event, attracting dozens of volunteers. By the end of the summer, they had removed hundreds of pounds of trash from the beaches, improving both the environment and the experience for local residents and tourists alike.

You don't need to start with something big. It could be as simple as joining an existing beach clean-up or helping out with a local tree-planting event. These small actions, when done consistently, add up to significant environmental change.

Tutoring and Mentoring At-Risk Youth

There's an urgent need for volunteers to support at-risk youth in communities across the country. Many children face challenges like poverty, unstable home environments, or learning disabilities, and a little extra help can make all the difference.

Think back to Theresa's story from earlier. She volunteered a few hours a week to tutor at-risk youth at her local library, and it made a lasting impact on the lives of those children. Tutoring doesn't require a degree in education—just patience, empathy, and a willingness to help.

Many schools, libraries, and community centers offer tutoring and mentoring programs where volunteers can provide academic support, career guidance, or simply be a positive role model. If you're passionate about helping young people, this is a great way to make a direct impact in your community.

Supporting Local Food Banks and Shelters

Another area where volunteers are desperately needed is in supporting food banks and homeless shelters. These organizations often operate on tight budgets and depend heavily on volunteers to help prepare and distribute food, organize donations, and provide services to those in need.

Sarah, a college student, started volunteering at a local food bank during the holidays. At first, she helped pack boxes of groceries for families, but over time, she got more involved, assisting with organizing food drives and even working on the bank's social media to encourage donations. Sarah's efforts helped the food bank keep its shelves stocked and provided vital resources to hundreds of families during the winter months.

If you're looking to make a tangible difference, volunteering at a food bank, shelter, or soup kitchen is one of the most direct ways to help those in need in your community.

Starting Small but Staying Consistent: How a Few Hours a Month Can Have a Lasting Impact Over Time

One of the biggest misconceptions about volunteering is that it requires a huge time commitment. The reality is, even just a few hours a month can make a significant difference, especially when you're consistent. The key to effective volunteering isn't necessarily about the amount of time you give—it's about showing up regularly and being reliable.

Let's go back to Jacob and his beach clean-up efforts. At first, he wasn't organizing large events. He was simply spending an hour or two on a Saturday morning picking up trash with a few friends. But because he did it consistently, over time, it grew into something much bigger. His small but regular effort inspired others to join in, and together, they made a noticeable improvement to their local environment.

Or think about Theresa. Two hours a week of tutoring doesn't sound like much, but for the children she worked with, it was the difference between falling behind and thriving in school. The impact of her small, regular effort rippled out in ways she couldn't have imagined.

Consistency also helps build relationships. Whether you're tutoring students, supporting a food bank, or volunteering with a local environmental group, showing up regularly allows you to develop deeper connections with the people and causes you're serving. It also makes you a trusted part of the organization, someone they can count on to help move their mission forward.

If you're worried about finding time to volunteer, start small. Maybe it's just one hour a month at first. Maybe it's a single Saturday spent at a beach clean-up or a few hours helping sort donations at a food drive. The important thing is to get started. As you find causes you're passionate about, you'll likely find that volunteering becomes something you look forward to, and over time, you might even find yourself giving more time than you expected.

The Power of Your Time

Volunteering your time is one of the most meaningful ways to make a difference, and the best part is that there's no one "right" way to do it. Whether you're tutoring virtually from home, organizing beach clean-ups in your community, or using your professional skills to help a nonprofit, your time is invaluable.

In a world where many problems feel too big to tackle, volunteering reminds us that small actions, done consistently, can lead to significant change. The hours you give, no matter how few, are an investment in a better, more just world. So, don't underestimate the power of your time—it's one of the greatest gifts you can offer.

CHAPTER 5: SKILL-BASED PHILANTHROPY

When we think of philanthropy, we often imagine giving money or donating time to volunteer for a cause. But there's another powerful form of giving that doesn't always get the spotlight it deserves: *offering your expertise*. Skill-based philanthropy is a way for professionals to make a direct, profound impact on the causes they care about by offering their specialized skills for free—whether you're a lawyer, accountant, web developer, or designer, your expertise can be invaluable to nonprofits and grassroots organizations that otherwise wouldn't have access to such services.

Let's be honest: many of us lead busy lives. We juggle careers, family, personal passions, and all the other demands of life. Finding time to volunteer or donate might seem impossible. But skill-based philanthropy offers a way to contribute meaningfully without disrupting your schedule. The beauty of this approach is that you can use what you already do—what you're *good* at—to support a cause. You don't need to learn a new skill or completely rearrange your life. You just need to offer your talents in service to those who need them most.

Offering Your Expertise: How Professionals Can Offer Pro Bono Services

Imagine this: A small nonprofit working to provide clean drinking water in developing countries is struggling with its finances. They don't have the funds to hire a full-time accountant, and their financial statements are a mess. Enter Kelly, an accountant with years of experience who offers to help on a pro bono basis. Kelly steps in to organize their books, prepare their tax filings, and help them create a budget that ensures their mission continues to run smoothly. In a few months, the nonprofit is back on track, financially stable, and able to focus on its mission rather than worrying about its finances.

Kelly didn't need to give money or spend hours doing work outside her expertise. She simply used her existing skills to help an organization that desperately needed them.

Pro Bono Work: What Is It, and Why Is It Important?

"Pro bono" is a Latin phrase meaning "for the public good." In the professional world, it refers to providing services for free to those who cannot afford them. Many industries encourage or even require pro bono work, especially in fields like law and medicine. However, you don't need to be a lawyer or doctor to offer your expertise to a cause—any professional skill can be valuable.

The truth is, nonprofits often operate on shoestring budgets, and hiring professionals for critical services—like legal advice, accounting, marketing, or tech support—can be out of reach. That's where you come in. By offering your skills for free, you're helping nonprofits keep their costs down while also allowing them to operate more effectively. You're giving them the tools they need to focus on what they do best: serving their mission.

Examples of Pro Bono Services Across Different Professions

1. Lawyers and Legal Services

Nonprofits, like any other organization, often deal with legal challenges, whether it's drafting contracts, dealing with employment law, or navigating complex regulations. Many small nonprofits simply can't afford to hire a lawyer, and this is where pro bono legal services can be a lifesaver.

Take the story of Jim, an attorney who specializes in intellectual property law. Jim volunteered his time to help a nonprofit that creates educational resources for children with disabilities. The organization was expanding its reach and creating new digital content, but they were worried about copyright issues and wanted to make sure their intellectual property was protected. Jim spent a few hours reviewing their contracts, offering advice, and setting up protections for their original content. His expertise helped the nonprofit avoid potential legal pitfalls, allowing them to continue their important work without fear of legal consequences.

If you're a lawyer, offering pro bono legal services can make a huge difference for nonprofits, small businesses, or individuals in need. Whether it's reviewing contracts, offering advice on compliance, or helping with disputes, your expertise is invaluable.

2. Accountants and Financial Advisors

Many nonprofits struggle to manage their finances effectively. They often operate with minimal financial oversight, which can lead to disorganized books, improper tax filings, and difficulty securing funding. As an accountant or financial advisor, you can help organizations navigate these challenges by offering your expertise in financial planning, tax preparation, or auditing.

Sarah, a financial advisor, volunteered her time to help a local homeless shelter create a sustainable financial plan. The shelter was reliant on inconsistent donations and was struggling to cover its monthly expenses. Sarah worked with the shelter's director to create a budget, implement a financial reporting system, and establish a plan for building an emergency fund. Within a year, the shelter was more financially stable and had even started saving for a future expansion. Sarah's expertise didn't just help the shelter in the short term—it set them up for long-term success.

3. Web Developers and Tech Support

In today's digital age, having a functional website and strong online presence is essential for any organization, including nonprofits. However, many smaller nonprofits lack the funds to hire professional web developers or tech support. As a web developer or IT professional, you can offer your skills to help them create or improve their websites, set up digital tools, or even provide cybersecurity support.

Consider the story of Ayesha, a web developer who wanted to give back but didn't know how. She volunteered her time to help a nonprofit that provided literacy resources to underprivileged children. The nonprofit's website was outdated and difficult to navigate, which was hindering their ability to attract donors and reach new families. Ayesha redesigned the website, making it more user-friendly and mobile-optimized. The new site attracted more visitors, boosted online donations, and allowed the nonprofit to expand its reach. What took Ayesha a few weeks of work made a long-lasting difference for the organization.

If you have tech skills, offering pro bono support to nonprofits can be transformative. Whether it's building a website, setting up email systems, or providing IT troubleshooting, your expertise can empower nonprofits to operate more efficiently and effectively.

4. Designers, Writers, and Creative Professionals

Nonprofits need creative professionals, too! From graphic designers to copywriters to photographers, creative skills are always in demand. Whether it's designing marketing materials, creating a brand identity, or writing compelling copy for a fundraising campaign, creative professionals have the power to help nonprofits tell their stories and connect with supporters in meaningful ways.

Take the example of Lisa, a graphic designer who volunteered her time to create a brand identity for a new nonprofit focused on mental health awareness. The nonprofit had a great mission, but they were struggling to build awareness and attract donations because they didn't have a consistent visual identity. Lisa worked with the team to design a logo, create a color scheme, and develop a set of marketing materials that helped the nonprofit stand out. With their new branding in place, the organization saw a spike in donations and event attendance, all thanks to Lisa's design skills.

If you're a creative professional, offering your expertise to a nonprofit can make their message more impactful and help them reach more people. Whether it's designing a logo, writing blog posts, or creating videos, your creativity can bring a nonprofit's vision to life.

DIY Philanthropy Projects: Practical Ways to Use Your Expertise

While offering pro bono services to existing organizations is a fantastic way to give back, you can also create your own DIY philanthropy projects. These are initiatives where you use your skills to directly serve a cause, often starting from scratch. The beauty of DIY philanthropy is that it gives you full control over how you apply your expertise, and it allows you to take ownership of a project from start to finish.

1. Building a Website for a Nonprofit or Grassroots Group

As we've already seen, many nonprofits and grassroots organizations lack the technical know-how or budget to create a professional website. If you have web development skills, you can offer to build a website for a cause you care about. This could be a local environmental group, a charity that supports refugees, or even a school in a developing country.

When Danielle, a web developer, wanted to get involved in the fight against climate change, she realized she could offer her skills to help local environmental organizations amplify their message. She reached out to a grassroots group that was working to protect wetlands in her area and offered to build them a website for free. The group had been relying on social media, but Danielle's website gave them a more professional platform to showcase their work, provide educational resources, and accept donations. The website also included an events calendar, making it easier for people to join clean-up efforts and advocacy events. Thanks to Danielle's initiative, the organization was able to expand its reach and grow its volunteer base.

If you're a web developer, consider reaching out to local nonprofits or grassroots groups and offering to build or improve their websites. It's a small effort on your part but can make a huge difference in their ability to operate.

2. Writing Grant Applications

Nonprofits rely heavily on grants to fund their programs, but writing grant applications can be a daunting and time-consuming process. If you have strong writing and research skills, offering to write or edit grant applications is one of the most impactful ways to support a nonprofit.

Consider the story of Marcus, a freelance writer who wanted to support a local homeless outreach program. He wasn't sure how to help at first, but after talking to the program director, he learned that they were struggling to secure grant funding. Marcus volunteered to help write grant applications, using his writing skills to craft compelling narratives that outlined the program's impact and goals. Within six months, the program received two major grants that allowed them to expand their services. Marcus's efforts didn't just raise money—they provided the nonprofit with the resources they needed to help more people.

If you're a strong writer or researcher, grant writing is an incredibly valuable skill to offer. Many nonprofits struggle with the grant process, and your expertise could be the key to helping them secure critical funding.

3. Offering Strategic Advice

Sometimes, what a nonprofit needs most isn't physical labor or donations—it's strategic guidance. Many nonprofits are started by passionate individuals who have a strong vision but lack business experience. If you have skills in management, business strategy, marketing, or fundraising, offering strategic advice can help nonprofits grow, become more sustainable, and achieve their long-term goals.

Sarah, a marketing executive, volunteered with a small nonprofit that provided after-school programs for low-income students. The organization was struggling to attract donations and didn't have a clear marketing strategy. Sarah offered her expertise, helping them create a long-term marketing plan that included social media outreach, email campaigns, and community partnerships. Within a year, the nonprofit's donations had doubled, and their programs were reaching more students than ever before.

If you have experience in business or marketing, offering strategic advice can help nonprofits operate more effectively and expand their reach. It's a way to give back that doesn't require a huge time commitment but has a lasting impact.

4. Organizing Workshops or Training Programs

Another great way to use your expertise is by organizing workshops or training programs for nonprofits, community groups, or underserved populations. If you're an expert in a particular field, sharing your knowledge can empower others and create lasting change.

For example, imagine you're an IT professional who organizes a series of free workshops teaching digital literacy to seniors or underprivileged youth. Or maybe you're a lawyer who offers free legal clinics to small businesses or low-income families. These workshops don't just provide immediate help—they build skills and confidence that participants can use long after the workshop ends.

James, a software engineer, did just that when he started offering free coding workshops at his local community center. His workshops were aimed at teenagers from low-income families who didn't have access to tech education at school. Over time, his workshops grew in popularity, and some of his students even went on to pursue careers in tech. What started as a small initiative became a gateway for young people to explore new opportunities.

If you have specialized knowledge or skills, consider organizing a workshop or training program. It's a way to give back that empowers others and leaves a lasting impact.

Making Your Skills Work for a Cause

The beauty of skill-based philanthropy is that it allows you to make a meaningful impact without stepping too far outside your day-to-day life. You don't need to make a major time commitment or give large sums of money—just offering your professional skills for free can be a game-changer for nonprofits and communities in need.

Whether you're a lawyer providing pro bono legal advice, a designer creating marketing materials, or a web developer building a website for a cause, your expertise is invaluable. And if you're looking for a more hands-on approach, DIY philanthropy projects like writing grants or organizing workshops allow you to take control of your impact and use your skills in creative ways.

So, what are you waiting for? You already have what it takes to make a difference. It's time to take those skills you've honed in your career and use them to support a cause you care about. By offering your expertise, you're not just helping an organization—

you're helping build a better world.

Part III: Out-of-the-Box Philanthropy

CHAPTER 6: CREATIVE FUNDRAISING

When we think about fundraising, it's easy to picture grand galas, black-tie dinners, or large-scale charity events. While these traditional forms of fundraising can raise significant sums of money, they also require big budgets, large venues, and lots of planning. But here's the good news: creative fundraising doesn't have to be grand or expensive to be effective. In fact, some of the most impactful fundraising efforts are grassroots, low-cost, and even a little unconventional.

In this chapter, we'll explore creative ways to fundraise—strategies that anyone can use, regardless of their financial resources. Whether you're an individual looking to support a cause you care about or part of a nonprofit organization seeking fresh fundraising ideas, there are countless ways to raise money that go beyond the traditional bake sale or raffle. Let's dive into four key approaches: micro-fundraising, purposeful events, viral social media challenges, and using minimalism as a tool for giving.

Micro-Fundraising for Impact: Crowdfunding and Using Platforms Like GoFundMe for Causes

Let's start with one of the most accessible forms of fundraising: micro-fundraising through crowdfunding platforms like GoFundMe, Kickstarter, or GlobalGiving. In today's digital age, anyone with an internet connection can launch a fundraising campaign in minutes. These platforms have revolutionized the way people raise money, allowing individuals and organizations to tap into their personal networks—and beyond—to support causes they care about.

The Power of Small Donations

You might wonder how much impact a small crowdfunding campaign can actually have. After all, we've been conditioned to think that fundraising success comes from large donations and wealthy benefactors. But micro-fundraising turns that notion on its head. It's not about one person giving a lot; it's about a lot of people giving what they can.

Take the story of Scott Harrison, founder of the nonprofit organization *charity: water*. Scott didn't come from a background in wealth or fundraising. He started with a simple idea: what if we could ask people to donate their birthdays? Instead of receiving gifts, people would ask friends and family to donate to clean water projects. This simple crowdfunding approach turned into a global movement. Thousands of people donated their birthdays, raising millions of dollars for clean water projects. And many of those donations were small—$10, $25, $50—but together, they added up to something monumental.

This is the power of micro-fundraising: it democratizes giving. You don't need a massive budget or influential connections to make a difference. You just need to tap into the collective power of small donations.

How to Run a Successful Crowdfunding Campaign

If you're new to crowdfunding, it can feel overwhelming. But with the right approach, it's a powerful tool for raising funds. Here's a step-by-step guide to get you started:

1. **Choose Your Platform**: There are many crowdfunding platforms to choose from, including GoFundMe, Kickstarter, Indiegogo, and GlobalGiving. Each platform has its own strengths, so choose the one that aligns

with your goals. For personal causes or small projects, GoFundMe is a great option. If you're raising funds for a nonprofit or global cause, GlobalGiving might be a better fit.

2. **Tell a Compelling Story**: Successful crowdfunding campaigns are built on storytelling. Donors want to know why they should care about your cause, and the more personal and compelling your story, the more likely people are to contribute. Be transparent about what the funds will be used for and how they'll make a difference. Don't be afraid to tug at the heartstrings—stories of real people and real impact resonate deeply.

3. **Set a Realistic Goal**: One of the keys to micro-fundraising success is setting a realistic goal. People are more likely to donate if they feel their contribution can help you reach a tangible target. Start with a modest goal, and if you surpass it, you can always raise it later.

4. **Leverage Your Network**: Crowdfunding works best when you tap into your existing network—friends, family, coworkers, and social media connections. Start by reaching out to your close circle and asking them to contribute and share. As more people donate and spread the word, your campaign will gain momentum.

5. **Express Gratitude**: Thank your donors—publicly and privately. Acknowledging every contribution, no matter how small, fosters goodwill and encourages others to give. You can also offer small perks or rewards for different donation levels, such as a personal thank-you note or shout-out on social media.

Crowdfunding is a simple but powerful way to fundraise for a cause you're passionate about. It shows that with enough people behind you, even the smallest donations can have a big impact.

Events with Purpose: Organizing Community Events Like Charity Yoga Classes, Dinner Parties, or Online Workshops

to Raise Awareness and Funds

If you're the type of person who loves bringing people together, organizing a community event is a fantastic way to fundraise. Whether it's an in-person gathering or a virtual event, hosting something with a purpose allows you to raise money while also fostering a sense of community and shared mission.

Charity Yoga Classes: Moving with Purpose

Let's take the example of Sarah, a yoga instructor who wanted to give back to her community. She decided to organize a series of charity yoga classes, where participants would donate whatever they could to attend. All proceeds went to a local homeless shelter. Sarah's classes weren't just about practicing yoga—they were about creating a space where people could contribute to something bigger than themselves while focusing on their own well-being.

The concept is simple but powerful: use something you already love doing—whether it's yoga, fitness, or another hobby—and turn it into a fundraising event. You don't need a fancy venue or a huge guest list. You just need a few willing participants and a cause to rally around.

Dinner Parties with a Cause

Another creative fundraising idea is to host a *dinner party with a purpose*. Imagine gathering a group of friends, family, or colleagues around your dining table (or virtually via Zoom) for a night of great food, conversation, and giving. Instead of asking for traditional donations, you can make the meal itself part of the cause—charge a "donation fee" for attending, or ask guests to contribute what they would have spent at a restaurant.

This is exactly what Jenna did when she wanted to support a local food bank. She hosted a series of "Dinner for a Cause" evenings, where guests would enjoy a homemade meal in exchange for a donation to the food bank. Jenna's events were casual, fun, and filled with meaningful conversation about food insecurity in her community. Over the course of a year, she raised thousands of dollars, all while enjoying time with friends and raising awareness for the cause.

Hosting a dinner party or gathering with purpose is a great way to engage your community, spark important conversations, and raise funds in a relaxed and enjoyable setting.

Online Workshops for Good

In today's digital world, online workshops are a fantastic way to fundraise while sharing your expertise. Whether you're a teacher, artist, or professional with a particular skill, you can offer an online class where participants donate to attend. The best part? It doesn't require a venue, travel, or a large budget—just your time and knowledge.

Take Mike, a professional photographer who wanted to raise funds for environmental conservation. He hosted a series of online photography workshops, teaching participants how to take stunning nature photos. Instead of charging a traditional fee, Mike asked for donations to an environmental nonprofit he supported. The workshops were a hit, raising awareness for conservation efforts while teaching a valuable skill.

If you have a skill or passion that you can share with others, consider hosting an online workshop as a way to raise funds. It's a low-cost, high-impact method to spread knowledge and support a cause.

Social Media Challenges: Launching Fun, Viral Challenges with a Message

Social media has revolutionized fundraising, allowing people to connect with causes in creative and often unexpected ways. One of the most exciting trends in recent years has been the rise of *social media challenges*—fun, viral activities that engage people around the world while raising money for a cause.

The Ice Bucket Challenge: A Viral Sensation

The most famous example of this is the Ice Bucket Challenge, which took the internet by storm in the summer of 2014. The challenge was simple: dump a bucket of ice water over your head, post the video online, and nominate others to do the same. Participants were also encouraged to donate to the ALS Association, which supports research for amyotrophic lateral sclerosis (ALS), also known as Lou Gehrig's disease.

What started as a fun, quirky challenge quickly turned into a global movement. Millions of people participated, from everyday citizens to celebrities and world leaders. The result? The ALS Association raised over $115 million in donations, and the challenge brought unprecedented attention to the disease.

Creating Your Own Social Media Challenge

You don't need to replicate the Ice Bucket Challenge to create a successful social media campaign. The key to launching a successful social media challenge is to make it fun, easy to participate in, and directly connected to your cause. Here's how to create one of your own:

1. **Make It Fun and Engaging**: The most successful social media challenges are those that people enjoy doing. It could be as simple as taking a fun photo, completing a challenge (like running a virtual marathon), or sharing a personal story. The activity itself should be easy to participate in and share.

2. **Connect It to Your Cause**: Make sure your challenge is clearly connected to the cause you're supporting. If you're raising funds for an environmental nonprofit, your challenge might involve picking up trash in your local park or planting a tree and sharing a photo. If your cause is related to mental health, you might encourage

participants to share one thing they do to maintain their well-being.

3. **Encourage Participation**: A successful challenge spreads through nominations. Just like the Ice Bucket Challenge, ask participants to tag their friends, family, or followers and encourage them to take part. This creates a ripple effect that helps the challenge go viral.

4. **Ask for Donations**: While not everyone will donate, be sure to include a link or instructions for how participants can contribute to the cause. Even small donations add up when many people get involved.

Social media challenges are a low-cost, high-impact way to raise awareness and funds while engaging people in fun and meaningful ways. You never know—your challenge could be the next viral sensation!

Minimalism for a Cause: Decluttering and Donating Proceeds from Sales

If you've ever looked around your home and thought, "I have way too much stuff," you're not alone. In recent years, minimalism has become a popular lifestyle movement, encouraging people to declutter their lives and live with less. But what if you could turn your decluttering efforts into a fundraising opportunity?

Garage Sales and Online Auctions

One of the simplest ways to fundraise through minimalism is by hosting a garage sale or selling your unwanted items online. Whether it's clothes, furniture, electronics, or collectibles, many of us have more than we need. By selling those items, you can turn clutter into cash—and donate the proceeds to a cause you care about.

Take the example of Rachel, who wanted to raise money for a children's hospital in her city. She decided to hold a garage sale, selling everything from clothes and toys to kitchen appliances.

Rachel's neighbors, friends, and family heard about the sale and began donating items to add to her inventory. By the end of the weekend, Rachel had raised over $1,000, which she donated directly to the hospital's fundraising campaign. Her clutter—and the clutter of her community—turned into much-needed support for a local cause.

If you don't want to host a physical garage sale, consider selling your items on platforms like eBay, Poshmark, or Facebook Marketplace. Many sellers choose to donate a portion (or all) of their sales to charity, turning their online marketplace into a tool for philanthropy.

Decluttering for Charity Auctions

Another creative way to give through minimalism is by participating in or organizing charity auctions. Many charities and nonprofits hold auctions where supporters can bid on items, and the proceeds go directly to the organization. If you have valuable or unique items that you no longer need, donating them to a charity auction can raise significant funds.

For example, when Zoe's local school was organizing an annual fundraising auction, she decided to donate some of her unused designer handbags. The bags were auctioned off to the highest bidders, raising over $500 for the school's arts program. Zoe's decision to declutter not only helped her simplify her life but also supported a cause close to her heart.

Thinking Outside the Box to Make a Difference

Creative fundraising is all about thinking outside the box. Whether you're crowdfunding through small donations, organizing events with a purpose, launching a viral social media challenge, or using your decluttering efforts to raise money, there are countless ways to make a difference without a big budget. The key is to tap into your passions, your creativity, and your network to find a fundraising method that works for you.

At the end of the day, it's not about how much you raise—it's about the impact you're able to make. And with a little creativity, you can turn even the smallest efforts into something meaningful for the causes you care about.

CHAPTER 7: EVERYDAY PHILANTHROPY

When most people hear the word "philanthropy," they often think of grand gestures—large donations to charity, global fundraising efforts, or significant contributions of time and money. But what if I told you that philanthropy isn't just for the wealthy or the well-connected? In fact, it's something we can all practice every day, in small but meaningful ways, as we go about our normal lives. That's the beauty of *everyday philanthropy*: you don't need to be a billionaire to make a difference; you just need a mindset of giving and a willingness to integrate that spirit into your daily routines.

This chapter is about finding those small, manageable ways to contribute to the causes you care about without having to drastically alter your lifestyle. From donating old clothes to making mindful purchases, every action, no matter how small, can have a ripple effect. So, let's dive in and explore how you can turn everyday moments into opportunities to give back and make the world a better place.

The Concept of "Everyday Giving": Integrating Giving into Your Daily Life

Have you ever noticed how much we tend to accumulate over time? Whether it's clothes that no longer fit, books we've already read, or gadgets we no longer use, our homes often fill up with things we no longer need. What if you could turn those excess items into meaningful contributions for people in need?

Donating What You Already Have

Take the story of Lisa, a mother of two who was doing her annual spring cleaning. As she went through her closets and storage, she realized she had boxes of clothes that her children had outgrown, toys they no longer played with, and household items that hadn't been used in years. Instead of throwing these things away, she decided to donate them to her local women's shelter. The items, which would have otherwise collected dust or ended up in a landfill, were gratefully accepted by families in need. What was a small act of decluttering for Lisa made a significant difference for the people who received her donations.

That's everyday giving: the simple act of looking at what you already have and asking, "Who could benefit from this?" Whether it's clothes, books, toys, or even food, there's always someone who could use what you no longer need.

Sharing What You Grow

Another great example of everyday philanthropy comes from an unexpected place—your garden. If you've ever grown your own vegetables or herbs, you know the joy of harvesting fresh produce. But sometimes, you end up with more than you can use. Instead of letting that surplus go to waste, consider sharing it with your neighbors or donating it to a local food bank.

Take Brian, an avid gardener who loves growing tomatoes, cucumbers, and peppers. Every summer, his backyard garden produces far more vegetables than his family can eat. Instead of letting them rot on the vine, Brian started sharing his excess produce with neighbors, coworkers, and a local shelter. He realized that something as simple as a bag of tomatoes could brighten someone's day and help provide healthy food to people who might not have access to fresh produce otherwise.

You don't need to have a green thumb to participate in this kind of everyday giving. Even if you don't grow your own food, you can still share what you have—whether it's an extra loaf of bread you baked or a bag of apples you bought in bulk. Sharing what you have, no matter how small, fosters a sense of community and generosity that's at the heart of everyday philanthropy.

Helping Neighbors in Small Ways

Everyday philanthropy isn't limited to donating physical goods. Sometimes, the most valuable thing you can give is your time or a simple act of kindness. One of the easiest and most impactful ways to practice everyday giving is by helping your neighbors. You don't need to be part of an official organization to make a difference in someone's life—you just need to be present and willing to lend a hand.

Consider the story of Margaret, a retired nurse who lives in a small suburban neighborhood. Every morning, she walks her dog around the block, and over time, she's gotten to know her neighbors. One day, she noticed that her elderly neighbor, Mrs. Jensen, was struggling to carry groceries into her house. Without hesitation, Margaret offered to help. That small act of kindness led to regular check-ins, where Margaret would stop by to see if Mrs. Jensen needed anything—whether it was a ride to a doctor's appointment or simply someone to talk to. For Mrs. Jensen, those small gestures made her feel less isolated, and for Margaret, it was a simple way to give back to her community.

Helping your neighbors doesn't require any special skills or a large time commitment. It could be as simple as offering to mow someone's lawn, babysitting for a friend in need, or bringing over a meal when someone is sick. These small acts of kindness are what build strong, compassionate communities—and they're a powerful form of everyday philanthropy.

Living More Sustainably: Small Changes with Big Impact

Another way to practice everyday philanthropy is by living more sustainably. The choices we make every day—what we buy, how we dispose of waste, and how we consume resources—can have a profound impact on the environment and the world around us. By making small, sustainable changes in our daily lives, we can contribute to a healthier planet and support environmental causes without even realizing it.

Reducing Waste

Let's start with something simple: reducing waste. Every time you choose to recycle, compost, or avoid single-use plastics, you're making a small but meaningful contribution to the planet. These small actions, when practiced consistently, add up over time and reduce the strain on landfills and natural resources.

Take the example of Emma, who decided to reduce her household's waste by starting a compost bin in her backyard. At first, it seemed like a small, insignificant step, but as the months went by, she realized just how much food waste her family had been throwing away. By composting, Emma was not only reducing the amount of waste sent to the landfill, but she was also creating nutrient-rich soil that she used in her garden. It was a win-win: less waste for the environment, and healthier plants for her family.

You don't have to start a full-scale composting operation to reduce waste. Small steps, like bringing reusable bags to the grocery store, using a refillable water bottle, or saying no to plastic straws, can make a big difference. The key is to make these small actions part of your everyday routine, so they become second nature.

Supporting Local Farmers

Another way to live more sustainably is by supporting local farmers and producers. When you buy locally grown food, you're not only getting fresher, healthier ingredients, but you're also reducing the carbon footprint associated with long-distance transportation. Plus, you're supporting local economies and small-scale farmers who are often more environmentally conscious than large industrial farms.

Consider the story of Maria, who lives in a small town with a weekly farmers market. At first, she would only stop by the market occasionally, picking up a few items here and there. But as she learned more about the benefits of buying locally, she made a conscious decision to do the bulk of her grocery shopping at the farmers market. Not only did she enjoy fresher, tastier food, but she also felt good knowing that her purchases were supporting local farmers and reducing the environmental impact of long-distance shipping.

Buying locally might seem like a small change, but it has a ripple effect that benefits both the environment and the community. By choosing to support local farmers, you're participating in everyday philanthropy that promotes sustainability and strengthens your local economy.

Making Environmentally Conscious Purchases

Living sustainably also means being mindful of the products you buy. Whether it's choosing eco-friendly cleaning products, buying clothing made from sustainable materials, or investing in energy-efficient appliances, the choices you make as a consumer can have a big impact on the environment.

Take the story of Jack, who was in the market for a new washing machine. Instead of just picking the cheapest option, Jack did his research and chose an energy-efficient model that used less water and electricity. While it cost a bit more upfront, Jack knew that it would save him money in the long run and reduce his household's energy consumption. For Jack, this was a form of everyday philanthropy—making a conscious decision to invest in something that was better for the planet.

Making environmentally conscious purchases doesn't have to be complicated or expensive. It's about making small, thoughtful decisions every day that contribute to a healthier planet. Whether you're choosing products with minimal packaging, opting for sustainable fashion, or investing in energy-saving appliances, these choices add up and make a difference over time.

Mindful Consumerism: Choosing Brands and Businesses That Align with Ethical, Environmental, or Humanitarian Causes

One of the most powerful ways we can practice everyday philanthropy is through mindful consumerism. Every time you make a purchase, you're casting a vote for the kind of world you want to live in. By choosing to support brands and businesses that align with your values—whether it's ethical labor practices, environmental sustainability, or charitable giving—you can turn everyday transactions into acts of philanthropy.

Shopping with a Purpose

Let's look at the example of Susan, who is passionate about fair trade and ethical labor practices. She's done her research and made a conscious decision to support companies that pay their workers fair wages and operate with transparency. Instead of buying fast fashion, she opts for clothing made by fair trade brands, even if it costs a little more. For Susan, every purchase is an opportunity to support businesses that align with her values and contribute to a more just and equitable world.

This is the essence of mindful consumerism: being intentional about where your money goes. Every dollar you spend has power, and by choosing to spend it on companies that prioritize ethics, sustainability, and social responsibility, you're making a difference.

Supporting Social Enterprises

Another great way to practice mindful consumerism is by supporting social enterprises—businesses that are designed to make a positive impact on society or the environment. These companies operate with a "triple bottom line" approach, focusing not just on profit, but also on people and the planet.

Take the story of Tom's Shoes, a company built on the "buy one, give one" model. For every pair of shoes sold, Tom's donates a pair to a child in need. It's a simple but effective way to integrate giving into a business model, and it allows consumers to make a difference with every purchase. By choosing to buy from companies like Tom's, you're supporting a business that is actively working to improve the world.

Social enterprises exist in many different industries, from clothing and footwear to food and household goods. By choosing to support these companies, you're participating in a form of everyday philanthropy that turns your spending into a force for good.

Researching and Supporting Ethical Brands

If you're new to mindful consumerism, it can feel overwhelming to know where to start. The key is to do your research and make small changes over time. There are many resources available that can help you find ethical and sustainable brands, including websites, apps, and certification labels like Fair Trade, B Corp, and Certified Organic.

For example, Lauren wanted to make more ethical choices when buying beauty products. She discovered a website that listed cruelty-free and eco-friendly beauty brands, and she made a conscious effort to switch to products that aligned with her values. Over time, she found new brands she loved, and her beauty routine became a way for her to support companies that prioritized sustainability and animal welfare.

Mindful consumerism is about progress, not perfection. You don't need to overhaul your entire lifestyle overnight. Start small, with one or two categories, and gradually make changes as you learn more. Every purchase you make with intention is a step toward a more ethical and sustainable world.

Everyday Philanthropy is Within Reach

Philanthropy doesn't have to be grand, and it doesn't have to require large sums of money or time. Everyday philanthropy is about integrating small acts of giving into your daily life, whether it's donating what you no longer need, sharing what you grow, making sustainable choices, or supporting ethical businesses.

These small actions, practiced consistently, add up to meaningful change. They create a ripple effect that touches the lives of others, supports the planet, and builds stronger communities. The beauty of everyday philanthropy is that it's accessible to everyone, regardless of income or resources. All it takes is a willingness to give in whatever ways you can, and the belief that even the smallest actions can make a big difference.

So, as you go about your daily life, remember that every moment holds the potential for generosity, kindness, and impact. Whether it's helping a neighbor, choosing a sustainable product, or donating an old pair of shoes, everyday philanthropy is within your reach. And in the end, it's these small, everyday acts of giving that help build a better, more compassionate world.

Part IV: Building Your Own Philanthropic Platform

CHAPTER 8: STARTING A PASSION PROJECT

Many of us have moments where we feel a deep pull toward a particular cause, a burning desire to do something that matters. But often, that spark fades as quickly as it comes, overwhelmed by the enormity of the world's problems and the seeming impossibility of making a real difference. But here's a secret: *you can start something that changes the world*, even if it begins with just you and no money. Every movement, every nonprofit, every successful charity started with a single person and an idea.

This chapter is for those who want to take that idea and turn it into action. Whether you've been dreaming of launching a small nonprofit, starting a community movement, or simply creating impactful content around a cause you care about, the process is more accessible than you might think. Let's walk through how to turn that spark into a flame and start your own philanthropic project from scratch, all while staying grounded in the belief that small actions can lead to big changes.

Launching a Small Nonprofit or Charity: Steps to Get Started with No Initial Funding

If you've ever thought about starting a nonprofit or charity, the idea might seem overwhelming—especially if you don't have any funding to begin with. But many successful nonprofits started exactly this way: with a passionate founder, a clear mission, and a shoestring budget. Let's break down how to get started, even with limited resources.

Step 1: Define Your Mission

The first and most important step in starting a nonprofit is defining your mission. What problem do you want to solve? What community or issue do you care deeply about? Your mission should be clear, focused, and actionable. It's what will guide you through the challenges and keep you grounded in your purpose.

Take the example of Blake Mycoskie, the founder of TOMS Shoes. His mission was simple: for every pair of shoes sold, another pair would be donated to a child in need. What started as a small idea grew into a global movement, but it all began with that clear and simple mission—something that anyone could understand and support. When crafting your mission, think about the change you want to see and the steps you can take to make it happen.

Step 2: Start Small

It's tempting to dream big right out of the gate, but the most sustainable nonprofits often start small and grow gradually. Focus on one achievable goal that aligns with your mission. If you want to support homeless families, for example, maybe your first project is organizing a single community dinner or clothing drive. If you're passionate about environmental conservation, start with a neighborhood clean-up or educational workshop. Small, tangible projects allow you to build momentum, gain supporters, and show results, all without needing a lot of upfront capital.

Consider Jane, a high school teacher who wanted to address food insecurity in her community. She didn't have the resources to start a full-scale nonprofit, so she began by organizing monthly community dinners at her local church. Word spread, and more people joined the effort, contributing food, supplies, and their time. What started as a small project eventually grew into a full-fledged nonprofit that now provides meals and support services to hundreds of families in her town. Jane's success story reminds us that starting small doesn't limit your impact—in fact, it's often the best way to begin.

Step 3: Leverage Your Skills and Network

When you're starting a nonprofit with no initial funding, it's essential to leverage what you already have: your skills, your passion, and your network. Take a look at the people around you —friends, family, colleagues, and community members. Who has skills that could support your cause? Maybe you know a graphic designer who can create a logo, a lawyer who can help you navigate the legal side of things, or a friend with a large social media following who can help spread the word. Don't be afraid to ask for help. People are often more willing to contribute than you might think, especially when they see how passionate you are about your cause.

Take Ben, for example, who wanted to start a nonprofit to provide educational resources to underprivileged children. He didn't have the money to print materials or organize workshops, but he did have a strong network of fellow teachers, many of whom donated their time to create lesson plans and volunteer at after-school programs. By tapping into his community's skills and passion, Ben was able to build a successful organization without the need for large financial backing.

Step 4: Fundraise Creatively

While starting with no funding is possible, at some point you'll likely need to raise money to support your projects. The good news is that you don't need a huge budget to run a nonprofit— especially if you're creative with your fundraising efforts.

One approach is to start small with crowdfunding campaigns. Platforms like GoFundMe or Kickstarter make it easy for individuals to raise funds for causes they care about, and even small donations can add up quickly when you reach enough people. Share your story, be transparent about where the money will go, and don't be afraid to ask your network for support.

Another option is to seek in-kind donations. Many businesses and individuals are willing to donate goods or services in lieu of money. For example, if you're organizing a community event, ask local restaurants to donate food, or reach out to businesses to sponsor materials or services. In-kind donations can help you stretch your budget further and allow people to contribute in ways that work for them.

Step 5: Stay Focused on Your Mission

As your nonprofit grows, it's easy to get distracted by new opportunities, projects, or requests. But staying focused on your mission will keep your organization grounded and prevent burnout. Revisit your original goal regularly and make sure that everything you do aligns with that mission. By staying true to your purpose, you'll build trust with your supporters and create a sustainable organization that continues to make a difference over time.

Creating Community Movements: How to Inspire and Mobilize Others Around a Cause

Maybe starting a formal nonprofit isn't for you, but you still feel called to lead a movement or rally your community around a cause. Creating a community movement doesn't require legal paperwork or a big budget—it just takes passion, organization, and the ability to inspire others.

Start with a Shared Vision

A successful community movement starts with a shared vision —a cause that resonates with others and inspires them to take action. This vision should be clear, inclusive, and something that people can easily rally around. For example, if your goal is to clean up a local park, frame it in a way that appeals to different community members. Maybe you focus on creating a safer, more beautiful space for families to enjoy, or maybe you emphasize environmental conservation. The more inclusive and relatable your vision, the more likely you are to attract a diverse group of supporters.

Take Clara, a university student who noticed the rise of plastic pollution in her city's parks and beaches. She started a small social media campaign encouraging her friends to join her in a weekend park clean-up. Clara's message was simple but powerful: "Let's make our city beautiful again." What began as a small effort with a few friends quickly grew as more people shared her message and joined her cause. By focusing on a clear, shared vision, Clara was able to mobilize her community to take meaningful action.

Use the Power of Storytelling

Storytelling is one of the most effective tools for building a movement. When people connect emotionally with a cause, they're more likely to get involved and stay engaged. Use personal stories—your own or others'—to illustrate why your cause matters and how it affects real people.

Consider how Malala Yousafzai used her own story to inspire a global movement for girls' education. Her personal experiences, shared in her speeches and writing, resonated with millions around the world and galvanized them to join her cause. While your story might not be as dramatic as Malala's, it can still have a profound impact. People respond to authenticity, so share why this cause matters to you and how others can help make a difference.

Rally Your Community with Simple, Actionable Steps

People want to help, but they often don't know how. One of the best ways to build a movement is by offering simple, actionable steps that anyone can take to contribute. Make it easy for people to get involved by organizing events, offering volunteer opportunities, or providing clear calls to action.

For example, imagine you're passionate about addressing food waste in your community. Instead of trying to solve the entire issue at once, you could start by organizing a "food rescue" program, where volunteers collect surplus food from restaurants and grocery stores and deliver it to local shelters. By offering a clear, actionable way for people to participate, you'll build momentum and encourage more people to join the movement.

Impactful Social Media Campaigns: How to Use Instagram, YouTube, and TikTok to Raise Awareness About a Cause You Care About

Social media has revolutionized the way we connect with others and share information, making it one of the most powerful tools for raising awareness and mobilizing support for a cause. With platforms like Instagram, YouTube, and TikTok, you can reach thousands (or even millions) of people with just a few clicks. But building an impactful social media campaign requires more than just posting; it's about creating content that resonates, engages, and inspires action.

Leverage Visual Storytelling

One of the biggest strengths of social media is its ability to convey powerful messages through visuals. Platforms like Instagram and TikTok are highly visual, and using photos, videos, and graphics can help bring your cause to life in ways that words alone can't. For example, if you're passionate about animal rescue, sharing photos and videos of the animals you're helping can create an emotional connection with your audience and inspire them to get involved.

Take the story of Jenna, who started an Instagram account to raise awareness about deforestation in the Amazon. She posted striking photos of the forest, shared stories of indigenous communities affected by deforestation, and created informative graphics explaining the issue. Her account quickly gained a following, and she used it to encourage people to sign petitions, donate to conservation organizations, and spread the word. By leveraging the power of visual storytelling, Jenna was able to reach a global audience and make a real impact on a critical issue.

Engage Your Audience with Challenges and Hashtags

One of the best ways to build engagement on social media is through challenges and hashtags. These allow your audience to participate in the movement by creating their own content, which helps spread your message even further.

A perfect example of this is the #TrashTag challenge, which encouraged people to pick up litter in their communities, take a before-and-after photo, and share it with the hashtag #TrashTag. The challenge went viral, inspiring thousands of people around the world to clean up their local parks, beaches, and streets. What made this challenge so successful was its simplicity—anyone could participate—and the immediate, visible results.

If you're starting a social media campaign, consider creating a unique hashtag or challenge that encourages your followers to take action and share their efforts. It's a great way to build community, raise awareness, and get people involved in a hands-on way.

Use Videos to Connect on a Deeper Level

While photos and captions are great for raising awareness, videos allow you to connect with your audience on a deeper, more personal level. Platforms like YouTube and TikTok are perfect for creating video content that tells a story, explains an issue, or showcases the impact of your work.

Consider how Greta Thunberg used videos of her climate strikes to inspire millions of people around the world to join the fight against climate change. Greta's simple, straightforward videos of herself protesting outside the Swedish parliament captured the attention of the media and the public, sparking a global movement of young people demanding climate action. Videos have a way of humanizing your cause and showing people the tangible impact of your work.

If you're starting a social media campaign, consider creating short, engaging videos that showcase your cause, share personal stories, or highlight the results of your efforts. It's a powerful way to build a connection with your audience and inspire them to take action.

Collaborations with Existing Charities: Partnering with Larger Organizations to Amplify Your Efforts

While starting your own movement or nonprofit is exciting, you don't have to go it alone. In fact, one of the best ways to amplify your impact is by partnering with existing charities or organizations that share your mission. Collaborating with established nonprofits allows you to leverage their resources, networks, and expertise while bringing your unique passion and skills to the table.

Find Organizations That Align with Your Mission

The first step in collaborating with a charity is finding organizations that align with your mission. Look for nonprofits that are already working in the area you're passionate about, whether it's environmental conservation, poverty alleviation, or education. Reach out to them and offer your support—whether that's through volunteering, fundraising, or organizing joint events.

For example, if you're passionate about clean water access, you could partner with organizations like Water.org or charity: water. By collaborating with a larger organization, you can tap into their existing infrastructure while contributing your own ideas and energy.

Offer Your Unique Skills

When partnering with an existing charity, think about what unique skills or resources you can bring to the table. Maybe you have graphic design experience and can help create promotional materials, or maybe you're great at organizing events and can coordinate a fundraiser. Whatever your talents, offering them to an established organization allows you to contribute in meaningful ways while learning from their experience.

Take Sarah, a marketing professional who wanted to support a local animal rescue organization. Instead of starting her own nonprofit, she reached out to the rescue and offered her marketing expertise. She helped them create a social media strategy, design brochures, and launch a fundraising campaign. By partnering with the rescue, Sarah was able to make a significant impact without starting from scratch.

Amplify Your Impact Through Joint Campaigns

One of the biggest benefits of collaborating with existing charities is the ability to amplify your impact through joint campaigns. By working together, you can reach a larger audience, pool resources, and create a more significant impact than you could alone.

For example, imagine you're passionate about reducing food waste, and you've started a local food rescue initiative. By partnering with a larger organization like Feeding America, you could organize a joint campaign that brings more attention to the issue and raises funds for both your initiative and the national organization. Joint campaigns allow you to benefit from the resources and reach of a larger organization while still contributing to your local community.

Building Your Own Philanthropic Platform

Starting your own philanthropic platform—whether it's a small nonprofit, a community movement, or a social media campaign—might seem daunting, but it's entirely possible, even with limited resources. The key is to start small, stay focused on your mission, and leverage the power of storytelling, social media, and collaboration to amplify your impact.

By following the steps outlined in this chapter, you'll be well on your way to turning your passion into action. Whether you're launching a nonprofit from scratch, building a community movement, or partnering with existing organizations, you have the power to create real, meaningful change. So go ahead—take that first step and start building your own philanthropic platform today. The world needs your passion, your creativity, and your commitment to making a difference.

CHAPTER 9: INFLUENCING CHANGE THROUGH EDUCATION

In every corner of society, education has been a catalyst for change. Whether through conversations around the dinner table, informative workshops at community centers, or viral content on the internet, the way we share knowledge can shape minds, shift perspectives, and inspire action. Education isn't just about classrooms and textbooks; it's about engaging with people, planting seeds of understanding, and empowering them to make informed decisions. This is how true change happens, one enlightened person at a time.

In this chapter, we'll explore how you can become a powerful advocate for the causes that matter most to you through education. Whether you're passionate about environmental conservation, social justice, or any number of other causes, your ability to educate others—whether one-on-one or through broader platforms like blogs, workshops, or podcasts—can amplify your impact and inspire others to take action.

Becoming an Advocate: How to Use Your Voice to Educate Others on Important Issues

The first step in influencing change through education is recognizing the power of your own voice. Too often, people feel like they need to be experts in order to speak out on important issues. But the truth is, anyone with a passion for a cause can become an advocate. Your voice has power, and your experiences and perspectives are valuable in educating others.

Using Your Story to Inspire Change

One of the most effective ways to educate others is by sharing your personal story. Stories connect us to one another on an emotional level. When people hear real-life experiences that resonate with them, they're more likely to feel motivated to learn more and get involved. Sharing your story is not just about telling people what you know—it's about showing them why the issue matters to you.

Take, for example, environmental activist Greta Thunberg. Greta's journey began as a single, determined girl holding a sign outside the Swedish parliament, demanding action on climate change. Her message wasn't born from being an expert on environmental policy, but from a deeply personal concern about the future of the planet. Greta used her voice, fueled by her experiences and fears about climate change, to educate and galvanize millions of people worldwide to take action. By simply sharing her story, she created a movement.

You don't have to be Greta Thunberg to influence change through your voice. Every one of us has a story to tell, and it's these personal stories that can ignite passion in others. Whether you've experienced injustice firsthand or have learned from the people around you, your story can serve as a powerful tool for educating others. Share your journey, your reasons for caring about a cause, and how you've taken action to address it. You'll be surprised at how many people are willing to listen and learn.

Simplifying Complex Issues

Many of the issues we care about are complex—whether it's climate change, systemic racism, or healthcare reform. One of the most valuable roles you can play as an advocate is to help make these complex topics more understandable for others. Simplifying these issues doesn't mean dumbing them down; it means presenting the information in a way that is accessible, relatable, and actionable.

Take the example of Bill Nye, the "Science Guy." Bill Nye has spent years educating people, particularly young audiences, on topics like climate change and renewable energy. What makes his approach so effective is his ability to break down complex scientific concepts into engaging, bite-sized lessons that anyone can understand. Through humor, metaphors, and visuals, Nye makes science approachable, showing that educating others doesn't have to be intimidating—it can be fun and relatable.

As an advocate, you can do the same. Take the big issues you care about and distill them into key points that are easy for others to grasp. For instance, instead of overwhelming someone with all the data about climate change, you might focus on one element —like the impact of single-use plastics on ocean pollution—and provide simple, actionable steps they can take to reduce their plastic use. By focusing on what people can understand and relate to, you'll help them feel empowered to take action, rather than overwhelmed by the enormity of the problem.

Leading Conversations and Engaging Others

Being an advocate doesn't mean you have to lecture people or constantly try to "convince" them of your point of view. In fact, the best advocates are those who listen just as much as they speak. Engaging others in meaningful conversations is one of the most effective ways to educate. Start by asking questions, listening to different perspectives, and finding common ground.

Consider the story of Jamal, a community organizer who was passionate about criminal justice reform. Rather than simply telling people what he thought, Jamal made it a point to listen to the concerns of his community members, especially those who didn't agree with him. He held informal "coffee chats" where people could come and share their thoughts, ask questions, and learn about the issues in a non-judgmental space. By creating a welcoming environment for dialogue, Jamal not only educated his community but also built trust and opened the door for deeper conversations.

As an advocate, you can create similar spaces for open dialogue —whether that's through one-on-one conversations, group discussions, or even social media interactions. The goal is to engage, not lecture, and to help people feel more informed and empowered to take action.

Host Informative Workshops or Talks: Sharing Your Knowledge and Building Awareness in Your Community

One of the most impactful ways to educate others is by hosting workshops or talks. These events allow you to share your knowledge, facilitate discussions, and bring people together around a common cause. Whether you're organizing a small gathering at your local community center or hosting a virtual webinar, workshops and talks provide a powerful platform for learning and engagement.

Identifying Your Audience

The first step in hosting an informative workshop or talk is identifying your audience. Who are the people you want to reach? Are they parents concerned about their children's education? Are they community members who want to learn more about sustainability? Once you've identified your audience, you can tailor your content to meet their needs and interests.

Take the story of Priya, a nutritionist who was passionate about teaching people how to cook healthy, affordable meals. She noticed that many families in her neighborhood were struggling to balance good nutrition with tight budgets, so she decided to host a series of free cooking workshops at her local library. The workshops were a hit—families not only learned how to make healthy meals, but they also left with practical tips they could implement at home. Priya's workshops helped her community become more health-conscious, and the feedback she received inspired her to expand the program to neighboring towns.

By identifying the needs of her audience, Priya was able to create a workshop that was both relevant and impactful. The same principle applies to any cause you care about—whether you're educating people about environmental conservation, social justice, or mental health awareness. Knowing your audience allows you to provide them with the tools and knowledge they need to take action.

Creating Engaging and Interactive Content

A successful workshop or talk isn't just about presenting information; it's about engaging your audience in a way that makes them feel connected to the topic. People learn best when they're actively involved, so think about how you can make your event interactive and participatory.

Consider the story of Ana, an environmental advocate who wanted to educate her community about reducing household waste. Instead of giving a standard lecture, Ana organized an interactive workshop where participants could bring items from home that they weren't sure how to recycle. She taught them how to properly dispose of each item, shared tips for reducing waste, and even helped participants create their own DIY cleaning products using natural ingredients. By making the workshop hands-on and practical, Ana left a lasting impression on her audience and empowered them to make changes in their own lives.

Whether you're hosting an in-person event or a virtual talk, think about ways to engage your audience. You might include group discussions, Q&A sessions, interactive demonstrations, or even a "challenge" for participants to take home. The more engaged people are, the more likely they are to remember what they've learned and apply it to their own lives.

Collaborating with Experts and Guest Speakers

If you're not an expert on the topic you want to educate others about, don't worry—collaborating with experts or guest speakers is a great way to bring credibility and depth to your event. Inviting a knowledgeable speaker can provide your audience with valuable insights, while also enhancing the overall impact of your workshop or talk.

Take the example of Diego, a young activist who wanted to raise awareness about immigration reform in his city. Rather than trying to cover the entire topic himself, Diego invited local immigration lawyers, advocates, and community leaders to speak at his event. Each speaker brought their own expertise and perspective, which enriched the discussion and provided attendees with a well-rounded understanding of the issue. The event not only educated the audience but also strengthened the community's network of advocates.

If you're planning a workshop or talk, think about who you could invite as a guest speaker or collaborator. Whether it's a local expert, a nonprofit leader, or someone with lived experience, bringing in other voices can add depth to your event and help build connections within your community.

Starting a Blog or Podcast: Using Content Creation as a Platform for Change

In today's digital age, content creation has become one of the most accessible and powerful ways to influence change. Blogs, podcasts, and other forms of online content allow you to reach a global audience, share your ideas, and build a community around the causes you care about. Whether you're passionate about environmental sustainability, social justice, or mental health awareness, starting a blog or podcast is a fantastic way to educate and inspire others.

Choosing Your Platform and Niche

The first step in starting a blog or podcast is choosing your platform and niche. What topics are you passionate about, and how can you bring a unique perspective to the conversation? Your niche doesn't have to be broad—in fact, focusing on a specific area can help you build a more engaged audience.

Take the example of Jenna, a sustainability advocate who started a blog called "Waste Less Living." Jenna's blog focused specifically on zero-waste living and offered practical tips for reducing household waste, from composting to reusable products. Over time, Jenna built a loyal following of readers who were interested in living more sustainably, and her blog became a go-to resource for eco-conscious individuals.

If you're starting a blog or podcast, think about the topics you're most passionate about and how you can provide valuable, actionable content for your audience. Whether it's educating people about a specific issue, sharing personal stories, or interviewing experts, your platform should reflect your unique voice and perspective.

Creating Consistent and Engaging Content

Consistency is key when it comes to building an audience for your blog or podcast. Whether you're posting weekly, bi-weekly, or monthly, make sure you're delivering content that keeps your audience engaged and coming back for more.

Take the story of Alex, who started a podcast called "Voices for Change" focused on social justice issues. Each week, Alex interviewed activists, community leaders, and experts on topics ranging from racial equality to economic justice. By consistently providing insightful interviews and thought-provoking discussions, Alex built a dedicated listener base and helped raise awareness about important issues. Over time, his podcast became a platform for marginalized voices to share their stories and advocate for change.

When creating content, think about how you can engage your audience and keep them interested. You might share personal stories, offer practical tips, or interview experts in your field. The key is to provide content that's both informative and inspiring, so your audience feels empowered to take action.

Amplifying Your Reach Through Social Media

Once you've started your blog or podcast, social media can be a powerful tool for amplifying your reach and building a community around your content. Platforms like Instagram, Twitter, and Facebook allow you to share your posts, engage with your audience, and connect with other advocates and organizations in your niche.

Take the story of Ellie, a climate change activist who used social media to grow her blog's audience. Ellie shared excerpts from her blog posts on Instagram, created visually appealing infographics about climate action, and used Twitter to engage with environmental organizations and activists. By leveraging social media, Ellie was able to build a strong online presence and grow her audience beyond her blog's immediate reach.

If you're starting a blog or podcast, be sure to use social media to your advantage. Share your content, engage with your audience, and collaborate with other advocates to amplify your message and expand your reach.

Empowering Change Through Education

Education is one of the most powerful tools we have for creating lasting change. Whether you're sharing your personal story, hosting a workshop, or starting a blog or podcast, your ability to educate others can inspire action and influence the world around you.

As an advocate, your voice matters. You don't need to be an expert or have a large platform to make a difference—you just need passion, persistence, and a commitment to sharing what you know. By becoming an educator in your own right, you'll not only raise awareness about the issues you care about but also empower others to take action and join the movement for change.

So, whether you're leading conversations in your community, organizing workshops, or creating digital content, remember that your efforts to educate can have a profound and lasting impact. It's through these everyday acts of education that we can create a more informed, compassionate, and just world.

CHAPTER 10: THE FEAR OF NOT BEING ENOUGH

We've all been there—that moment when you want to make a difference, but a nagging voice in your head whispers, *"What can one person really do?"* It's easy to feel overwhelmed by the enormity of the world's problems—climate change, poverty, inequality—and feel like your individual efforts won't matter. You might think, "I'm just one person, with limited time, resources, and influence. How can I possibly make a dent in these massive issues?"

This feeling—that your contributions aren't enough—is a common obstacle for anyone who wants to get involved in philanthropy or activism. And yet, history is filled with examples of how small actions by individuals have sparked significant change. In this chapter, we'll explore how to overcome the fear of not being enough, confront imposter syndrome, and learn to trust that even your smallest contributions can create ripple effects that matter.

"What Can One Person Really Do?": Overcoming the Feeling That Individual Contributions Are Insignificant

One of the most powerful forces holding people back from getting involved in causes they care about is the feeling that individual efforts won't make a real difference. You may look at the scale of the problem and think, "This is too big for me to solve." But here's the truth: *change always starts with individuals.*

Small Actions, Big Impact: The Ripple Effect of Individual Efforts

Take the story of Jadav Payeng, an environmental activist from India who, for decades, planted trees in a barren patch of land near his home. He started this journey alone, without fanfare or large-scale support. Every day, he planted a few trees, nurturing them as they grew. Over time, his daily efforts transformed what was once a desolate area into a 1,300-acre forest, now home to wildlife like elephants and tigers. Jadav's story is proof that small, consistent actions can create massive change, even when it feels like you're working alone.

What Jadav did was monumental, but he didn't start with a grand plan or a huge organization behind him. He started with one small act—planting a single tree. And that's something we can all learn from: change doesn't happen overnight or through one big action. It happens through countless small actions, repeated over time, that add up to something much bigger.

The Power of One Voice: How Individual Advocacy Can Inspire Movements

Consider the story of Malala Yousafzai, who became a global advocate for girls' education after being shot by the Taliban for attending school. At the time, Malala was just a young girl with a deep desire to go to school, but her personal story and courageous stand resonated with millions around the world. Her voice sparked a global movement for education equality, leading to the creation of the Malala Fund and countless initiatives that continue to fight for girls' right to education. What started as a single person's fight for her own education became a global call to action.

The key takeaway here is that one person, no matter how young, unknown, or ordinary they might feel, can influence massive change. Malala didn't have power, wealth, or a global platform when she started; she had her story and her voice, and that was enough to inspire millions.

When you find yourself asking, "What can one person really do?" remember that all big movements start with small actions. Even if it feels like you're just one drop in the ocean, every drop counts. The important thing is to begin, no matter how small the step.

Imposter Syndrome in Philanthropy: How to Silence Self-Doubt and Act, No Matter Your Experience Level

For many people who want to get involved in philanthropy or social activism, imposter syndrome can be a significant obstacle. Imposter syndrome is the feeling that you're not qualified or experienced enough to contribute to a cause. You might think, "Who am I to take a stand on this issue?" or "I don't have the expertise to make a difference." But the truth is, everyone starts somewhere, and the most important qualification is *caring* about the issue.

"I'm Not an Expert": Overcoming the Need for Perfection

Many people hold themselves back from taking action because they believe they need to be experts before they can contribute. But here's the thing: passion often matters more than expertise. You don't need to have a degree in environmental science to start advocating for sustainability. You don't need to be a healthcare professional to raise awareness about public health issues. What you need is the willingness to learn, engage, and take action.

Take the example of Jamie Margolin, a climate activist who co-founded the youth-led climate organization Zero Hour at the age of 16. Jamie didn't wait until she had years of experience or an advanced degree in environmental science. She saw the urgency of the climate crisis and decided to take action, rallying other young people to demand change. Her story reminds us that you don't need to be a seasoned expert to make a difference—you just need the courage to act.

If you find yourself doubting your qualifications or feeling like you're not "enough" to contribute, remind yourself that every expert was once a beginner. The key is to start where you are, with what you know, and be open to learning as you go.

Taking Action Before You Feel Ready

Another common symptom of imposter syndrome is the feeling that you're not ready to take action. You might think, "I need to learn more before I get involved," or "I'll start volunteering once I feel more confident in my knowledge." But waiting until you feel 100% ready often means waiting forever. The reality is, no one ever feels completely ready, and the only way to gain confidence is by taking that first step, no matter how uncertain you feel.

Consider the story of Sophie, a young woman passionate about mental health advocacy. She wanted to start a support group for people struggling with anxiety and depression, but she felt overwhelmed by the thought of leading a group. She wasn't a therapist, and she worried she didn't have the expertise to help others. But after speaking with a few friends who shared her struggles, Sophie realized that she didn't need to be a mental health professional to create a space for people to connect, share, and support one another. She took the plunge, started the group, and quickly found that her personal experience and empathy were enough to make a difference.

The lesson here is that sometimes, you have to act before you feel ready. Trust that your passion, compassion, and willingness to help are enough to get you started. You can learn and grow as you go, but the important thing is to take that first step.

Embracing the Value of Lived Experience

One of the most powerful ways to combat imposter syndrome is by embracing the value of your lived experience. Whether you've faced personal struggles, witnessed injustice, or simply have a deep connection to a particular cause, your experience is valid and valuable. Lived experience often provides a unique perspective that experts or professionals may not have.

Take the example of Tarana Burke, the founder of the #MeToo movement. Tarana started the movement based on her own lived experience as a survivor of sexual violence. At first, she wasn't a high-profile activist or a celebrity—she was a woman with a story, a cause, and a deep desire to create change. By sharing her story and creating a space for others to do the same, she ignited a global conversation about sexual harassment and assault that continues to influence policy and social change.

Your lived experience can be just as powerful. Whether you've experienced inequality, environmental degradation, or personal hardship, your perspective gives you insight and empathy that can drive meaningful change. Don't discount the value of your experiences—they are a crucial part of the movement you want to build.

Shifting the Narrative: From "I'm Not Enough" to "I'm Exactly What's Needed"

So, how do we shift our mindset from "I'm not enough" to "I'm exactly what's needed"? It starts with changing the way we think about our role in the larger picture of philanthropy and social change. Instead of focusing on all the ways we feel unqualified or insignificant, we can focus on the strengths we bring to the table —our passion, our unique experiences, and our ability to connect with others.

Start Small and Build Momentum

One of the most effective ways to combat the fear of not being enough is by starting small. You don't need to launch a major nonprofit or lead a massive protest on your first day. Instead, focus on taking one small action that aligns with your passion. Maybe that's signing a petition, organizing a community clean-up, or attending a local event. These small steps build momentum, and over time, you'll gain confidence in your ability to contribute.

Take inspiration from Wangari Maathai, a Kenyan environmental and political activist who founded the Green Belt Movement. Wangari didn't start her movement with grand ambitions to transform her country's landscape. Instead, she began by encouraging women in her community to plant trees as a way to combat deforestation and erosion. This simple act of tree-planting grew into a movement that resulted in the planting of over 50 million trees, improved livelihoods, and won her the Nobel Peace Prize. Wangari's story shows that small, consistent actions can grow into something far greater than you ever imagined.

Celebrate Progress, Not Perfection

It's easy to fall into the trap of feeling like you're not doing enough, especially when the problems you care about seem so large and urgent. But remember, it's not about being perfect or solving everything at once—it's about making progress. Every step you take, no matter how small, is moving you closer to the change you want to see.

Take the story of Susan, who started volunteering at a local animal shelter once a week. At first, she felt like her contributions were insignificant—after all, she wasn't solving the issue of animal homelessness on her own. But over time, Susan realized that her efforts, though small, were making a difference. She helped dozens of animals find loving homes and raised awareness about animal adoption in her community. Her work wasn't about achieving perfection—it was about making a positive impact, one animal at a time.

Celebrate your progress, no matter how small. Whether you're raising awareness, educating others, or contributing your time and skills, every action matters. It's the collective effort of individuals like you that creates lasting change.

Lean on Community and Collaboration

One of the most powerful ways to overcome the fear of not being enough is by recognizing that you're not in this alone. Philanthropy and activism are collective efforts, and you're part of a larger community of people working toward the same goals. When you collaborate with others—whether through volunteering, advocacy, or community organizing—you amplify your impact and feel supported in your efforts.

Consider the story of Bryan Stevenson, a public interest lawyer and the founder of the Equal Justice Initiative (EJI), which fights for criminal justice reform. Bryan has spent decades working to challenge racial and economic injustice, often taking on monumental cases and advocating for people on death row. While his work has been incredibly impactful, Bryan has always emphasized the importance of community and collaboration. He frequently speaks about the role that ordinary people play in advancing justice—whether through donating, volunteering, or raising awareness. Bryan's story reminds us that change is a team effort, and when we work together, we can accomplish far more than we could alone.

Remember Your "Why"

When self-doubt creeps in and you start questioning whether your efforts are enough, return to your "why"—the reason you got involved in the first place. What is it about this cause that moves you? What kind of change do you hope to see in the world? By grounding yourself in your purpose, you'll find the motivation to push past feelings of inadequacy and take action.

Take the story of Rosa Parks, whose refusal to give up her bus seat became a defining moment in the Civil Rights Movement. Rosa wasn't a public figure at the time—she was an ordinary woman with extraordinary courage. But what drove her to take that stand was her deep sense of justice and her belief in equality. Rosa's "why" gave her the strength to act, even in the face of fear and uncertainty.

Your "why" is what will keep you moving forward, even when you're unsure of yourself. It's the core of your passion, and it's what makes you exactly what's needed in the fight for change.

You Are Enough

Overcoming the fear of not being enough in philanthropy and activism is a journey. It's natural to feel small in the face of big challenges, and it's common to doubt your abilities. But remember this: you *are* enough. Your passion, your voice, your small actions—these are the building blocks of change. The world needs people like you who care, who are willing to take action, and who understand that even the smallest contribution can spark a ripple effect of goodness.

So the next time you find yourself asking, "What can one person really do?" or doubting your worth, remember the stories of people like Jadav Payeng, Malala Yousafzai, and Wangari Maathai. They all started with small, individual actions—actions that grew into movements that changed the world.

You don't have to have all the answers or be an expert. You just have to be willing to start. Because when you do, you'll find that your contributions are not only enough—they are essential.

CHAPTER 11: WHEN TIME IS LIMITED

In today's fast-paced world, the biggest obstacle many people face when it comes to philanthropy isn't a lack of passion or desire —it's time. Between work, family, and personal responsibilities, finding the hours to contribute to a cause can feel nearly impossible. You may often find yourself asking, "How can I make a difference when my schedule is already full?"

The good news is, making an impact doesn't always require huge blocks of time. In fact, many people with the busiest schedules find creative, meaningful ways to give back without overwhelming themselves. This chapter is all about balancing your schedule with purpose and incorporating philanthropy into your daily life—whether you're working, parenting, or pursuing other goals. You'll find that even with limited time, there are plenty of ways to make a difference.

Balancing Your Schedule with Purpose: Tips for Making Space in Your Life for Philanthropy Without Overwhelming Yourself

One of the most common misconceptions about philanthropy is that it requires large chunks of time. Many people think they need to volunteer for hours each week, attend frequent meetings, or run entire charity events to make a meaningful contribution. But philanthropy is not all-or-nothing. You can start small and still have a significant impact without adding stress to your already busy life.

1. Start by Identifying Your "Philanthropic Sweet Spot"

The first step in balancing your schedule with purpose is to find your *philanthropic sweet spot*—the intersection between your passions, your skills, and your available time. This sweet spot will allow you to make the most meaningful contributions without feeling stretched thin.

Take Sarah, for example, a full-time working mom with two young children. Sarah is passionate about education but has limited time to volunteer. Rather than trying to fit in traditional volunteering hours at a local school, she found a creative solution that fits her schedule: she uses her graphic design skills to create promotional materials for an educational nonprofit. She can work from home, on her own time, while still making a meaningful contribution to a cause she cares deeply about.

Your philanthropic sweet spot may look different from Sarah's. It could be using your professional skills in a freelance capacity for a nonprofit, hosting online events, or finding micro-volunteering opportunities that take just a few minutes at a time. The key is to align your contributions with your skills and passions in a way that fits your life.

2. Set Small, Realistic Goals

One of the biggest barriers to getting started in philanthropy is the feeling that you need to do something big to make a difference. This kind of thinking can lead to paralysis—if you can't devote hours to a cause, you might feel like it's not worth doing at all. But this couldn't be further from the truth. The key to balancing your schedule with purpose is setting small, realistic goals that are achievable with the time you have.

Take Ryan, a busy executive who wanted to get involved in his community but couldn't find the time for traditional volunteering. He started by setting a small goal: dedicating just 30 minutes each week to writing letters for a local campaign advocating for housing rights. It wasn't a huge time commitment, but over time, those 30 minutes added up, and Ryan became a consistent contributor to the cause. He didn't need to overhaul his life or make a major time sacrifice—he just needed to start small and stay consistent.

When thinking about how to fit philanthropy into your busy schedule, set small, attainable goals. Whether it's donating one hour a month, participating in a monthly online activism event, or committing to a few minutes a week on a cause, those small contributions add up. The key is consistency, not quantity.

3. Create "Philanthropy Blocks" in Your Schedule

For many people, the best way to balance their schedule with purpose is to create dedicated "philanthropy blocks" in their calendar. Just as you would schedule a meeting or a workout, setting aside specific time for philanthropic activities helps ensure that it doesn't fall by the wayside.

Jessica, a small business owner, struggled to find time for giving back. Her days were consumed with managing her business, and her weekends were reserved for family. But Jessica was determined to integrate philanthropy into her life, so she blocked out 30 minutes every Friday morning to research charities and make micro-donations to causes she cared about. By scheduling this dedicated time, Jessica ensured that her philanthropic efforts were part of her regular routine without overwhelming her already packed schedule.

If you feel like your week is too busy to add anything extra, try creating small philanthropy blocks in your schedule. These blocks don't need to be long—15 or 30 minutes is often enough to make a meaningful contribution. Whether it's volunteering, donating, or simply educating yourself about a cause, scheduling the time ensures that philanthropy becomes a regular part of your life.

4. Learn to Say "No" to Overcommitment

One of the biggest challenges in balancing your schedule with purpose is learning when to say no. It's easy to feel guilty for not doing more, especially when there are so many worthy causes that need attention. But overcommitting yourself can lead to burnout and reduce the effectiveness of your contributions.

Take Mia, a nonprofit consultant, who was constantly being asked to volunteer for various causes, speak at events, and join new initiatives. While Mia was passionate about many of these opportunities, she quickly found herself overwhelmed and struggling to balance her professional and personal life. After realizing that she couldn't give her best effort to everything, Mia decided to focus on two causes that were closest to her heart: supporting women entrepreneurs and advocating for environmental sustainability. By saying no to other commitments, Mia was able to give her full energy to the causes she cared about most.

Remember, it's okay to say no to causes or commitments that don't align with your top priorities or available time. Saying no allows you to focus on the areas where you can make the biggest impact and avoid spreading yourself too thin.

Incorporating Philanthropy into Daily Life: How to Seamlessly Integrate Giving into Your Everyday Routine

Balancing your time doesn't always mean carving out large chunks of your schedule for philanthropic efforts. Often, the most sustainable way to give back is by integrating philanthropy into your daily life. By weaving small acts of giving into your routine, you can make a significant impact without adding extra pressure to your already busy schedule.

1. Turn Your Commute into a Time for Advocacy

If you spend time commuting to work, running errands, or even walking the dog, this can be a perfect opportunity to engage in advocacy without requiring additional time. Listening to podcasts about social justice, environmental issues, or other causes you care about can be an easy way to stay informed and become a more effective advocate.

Take Lucas, who works in IT and has a long commute each day. Lucas wanted to learn more about climate change but struggled to find time in his schedule for extra reading. Instead of trying to squeeze in reading time, Lucas turned his commute into an opportunity to listen to podcasts on climate activism. Over time, this became his daily routine, and he found himself far more informed and engaged with the issue, all without needing to find extra hours in the day.

By using your commute or downtime to learn more about the causes that matter to you, you'll stay informed and connected, which can lead to greater advocacy efforts without taking time away from your other commitments.

2. Make Charitable Giving Part of Everyday Transactions

Another simple way to incorporate philanthropy into your daily life is by making charitable giving part of your regular transactions. Many apps and websites now allow you to round up your purchases to the nearest dollar and donate the difference to a charity of your choice. These small, automatic contributions can add up over time and provide ongoing support to causes you care about without any additional effort on your part.

Take Tasha, who signed up for an app that rounds up her debit card purchases and donates the spare change to a nonprofit focused on clean water access. Every time she buys groceries, fills up her car with gas, or grabs a coffee, a few cents are donated to the cause. Over the course of a year, those small amounts added up to a significant donation, and Tasha didn't have to make any major changes to her routine.

By setting up automatic donations or finding ways to

integrate giving into everyday purchases, you can contribute to philanthropy consistently, even when time is limited.

3. Get Your Family Involved

If you're balancing a busy family life, incorporating philanthropy into your routine can be a great way to teach your children about giving back while spending quality time together. Volunteering as a family or incorporating small acts of kindness into your daily activities helps instill values of compassion and generosity in your children while making a positive impact.

Consider the story of Julie and Rob, parents of two young children who wanted to introduce philanthropy into their family's routine. Every month, they dedicate one Saturday morning to a family volunteering activity, whether it's cleaning up a local park, preparing meals at a food bank, or organizing a clothing drive in their neighborhood. These activities not only create special family memories but also help their children understand the importance of giving back.

If you're a parent, think about how you can involve your family in philanthropy. It doesn't have to be a big event—small acts like helping a neighbor, donating toys to a children's charity, or even discussing important issues at the dinner table can make a difference while teaching valuable lessons.

4. Leverage Your Workplace for Good

Many workplaces now offer opportunities for employees to give back through company-sponsored volunteer days, donation matching programs, or partnerships with local charities. If your workplace offers these kinds of programs, take advantage of them as a way to incorporate philanthropy into your daily life without needing to find extra time outside of work.

Take Robert, a financial analyst whose company offers paid volunteer days each year. Robert uses these days to volunteer at a local youth mentoring program. Since it's part of his work schedule, he doesn't have to worry about fitting in extra time on weekends or evenings, and he's still able to contribute meaningfully to a cause he cares about.

If your workplace doesn't offer formal programs, consider starting one. Speak with your HR department or leadership about organizing a company-wide volunteer day or implementing a donation-matching program. This is a great way to involve your colleagues in giving back while making philanthropy a natural part of your work life.

5. Incorporate Philanthropy into Your Hobbies

One of the easiest ways to integrate philanthropy into your life is by combining it with something you already love doing. Whether it's running, baking, crafting, or any other hobby, there's almost always a way to incorporate giving into your passions.

Take the example of Paul, an avid runner who wanted to raise money for a charity that supports veterans. Instead of asking for donations directly, Paul decided to turn his love of running into a fundraiser. He set up a virtual charity run, where friends and family could pledge donations based on how many miles he ran each month. Not only did this allow Paul to raise funds for a cause he cared about, but it also motivated him to stay active and do something he loved.

Whatever your hobby, think about how you can use it to give back. Whether it's organizing a charity bake sale, knitting hats for a local homeless shelter, or hosting a crafting workshop for kids, integrating philanthropy into your passions makes it easy to contribute without feeling like you're taking on extra work.

Making Philanthropy Work for You

When time is limited, it's easy to feel like there's no room for philanthropy in your life. But the truth is, giving back doesn't have to be an overwhelming commitment. By finding ways to balance your schedule with purpose and seamlessly integrating philanthropy into your daily routine, you can make a meaningful difference without sacrificing your other responsibilities.

Whether it's setting small goals, leveraging your skills, involving your family, or combining philanthropy with your hobbies, there are countless ways to contribute to the causes you care about—even when your schedule is full. The key is to find what works for you, make it part of your routine, and remember that every small action counts.

You don't have to wait until you have more time. Start now, in whatever way you can, and watch how those small acts of kindness, generosity, and passion begin to add up. Because when it comes to making a difference, it's not about how much time you have—it's about how you use the time you've got.

CHAPTER 12: STAYING INSPIRED AND PREVENTING BURNOUT

Making change—real, tangible change—takes time. Whether you're fighting for environmental justice, advocating for the rights of marginalized communities, or working on the frontlines of humanitarian efforts, the journey can be long and exhausting. You might start with boundless energy and enthusiasm, but eventually, even the most passionate people can feel drained, discouraged, or burnt out when progress seems slow, or the challenges ahead feel insurmountable.

In this chapter, we're going to talk about how to stay inspired and motivated when the work feels tough and the results seem distant. We'll also explore the importance of finding a community of like-minded people to keep you going. No one makes lasting change alone, and your ability to sustain your impact depends on the support system you build around you.

Fueling Your Passion: How to Stay Energized and Motivated When Making Change Feels Slow

If you've ever planted a garden, you know that growth takes time. You plant the seeds, water them, give them sunlight, and wait. At first, it seems like nothing is happening. Days pass, then weeks, and there's no visible sign of change. But beneath the surface, those seeds are slowly taking root. Eventually, tiny shoots begin to break through the soil, and with consistent care, they grow into something beautiful and strong.

The same is true for change. Often, the progress we're making isn't immediately visible. It can feel like all our efforts are going unnoticed, like we're pouring ourselves into a cause and seeing little in return. But just like in the garden, the roots of change are taking hold beneath the surface, even when we can't see them.

1. Recognize the Power of Small Wins

When progress feels slow, one of the most important things you can do is recognize and celebrate small wins. These small victories may not seem like much in the grand scheme of things, but they are building blocks for larger success. When you start to notice and appreciate them, it's easier to stay motivated and keep going.

Take the story of Alana, an activist working to reduce food waste in her city. Alana spent months organizing community events, running social media campaigns, and petitioning local businesses to reduce their waste. For a long time, it felt like her efforts were falling flat. Businesses were slow to respond, and the community seemed indifferent to the cause. But one day, a small café in her neighborhood reached out and committed to donating its leftover food to a local shelter. That one small change sparked a ripple effect. Other businesses saw the café's success and followed suit, and soon, Alana's community was making noticeable strides in reducing food waste.

At first, Alana's progress felt slow and almost invisible, but by celebrating that first small win, she found the motivation to keep going. Small wins are proof that your efforts matter. They build momentum, create confidence, and remind you that change is happening—even if it's not as fast or as large as you initially hoped.

2. Reconnect with Your Purpose

One of the most powerful ways to stay inspired when the work feels slow is to reconnect with your purpose—the reason you started this journey in the first place. Why does this matter to you? What drives you to keep showing up, even on the hardest days?

Let's look at the story of Karim, a volunteer with an organization that provides free legal aid to refugees. After years of working long hours and facing constant bureaucratic hurdles, Karim began to feel overwhelmed. The victories felt few and far between, and the emotional toll of seeing families struggle to gain asylum wore him down. One day, he sat down with a refugee family he had helped years before, who now had legal residency and stable jobs. They shared how Karim's help had completely changed the course of their lives. It was a powerful reminder of why he started this work in the first place: to make a difference in the lives of people who had no other support.

Reconnecting with your "why" is crucial to keeping your passion alive. When you feel discouraged, take a moment to reflect on the people you're helping, the future you're working toward, and the change you believe in. This purpose will be your anchor in difficult times, helping you to stay grounded and energized when the path forward feels unclear.

3. Embrace Rest as Part of the Process

In a world that celebrates constant productivity, it can feel counterintuitive to rest when you're working toward an important cause. But the truth is, rest is an essential part of sustaining your impact. Without it, you risk burning out, losing your passion, and becoming ineffective in your efforts.

Consider the story of Lily, a passionate climate activist who was deeply involved in organizing protests, attending rallies, and lobbying for policy changes. For months, she barely took a day off, believing that if she wasn't constantly working, she was failing the cause. But eventually, Lily hit a wall. She was physically exhausted, emotionally drained, and struggling to find joy in the work that once energized her. Realizing that she couldn't keep going at that pace, Lily took a step back. She spent a few weeks resting, reconnecting with friends, and focusing on activities that brought her joy outside of activism. When she returned to her work, she felt rejuvenated and more capable than ever.

Rest isn't a sign of weakness—it's a necessary part of the process. Taking time to recharge allows you to return to your work with fresh energy, creativity, and resilience. If you're feeling burnt out, give yourself permission to rest. The cause will still be there when you're ready, and you'll be better equipped to contribute in a meaningful way.

4. Focus on What's Within Your Control

One of the fastest ways to burn out is to take on more than you can handle, especially when you're working on complex, global issues like climate change, social justice, or poverty. It's easy to feel overwhelmed by the enormity of the challenges and powerless in the face of such widespread problems. But the key to preventing burnout is focusing on what's within your control.

Take the example of Michelle, a teacher who was deeply concerned about inequality in education. At first, Michelle tried to tackle the issue on a broad scale, writing policy proposals, speaking at conferences, and engaging in national debates about education reform. But over time, she realized that the enormity of the issue was taking a toll on her mental health. She felt like no matter how hard she worked, she wasn't making a dent in the larger system.

So, Michelle shifted her focus. Instead of trying to solve the entire problem at once, she zeroed in on what she could control: the students in her classroom. She started organizing after-school tutoring sessions for students who needed extra help, partnered with local businesses to provide supplies, and advocated for her school to adopt more inclusive curricula. By focusing on her immediate sphere of influence, Michelle found renewed energy and satisfaction in her work.

You may not be able to change the world overnight, but you *can* make a difference in the people and communities around you. By narrowing your focus to what's within your control, you'll feel more empowered and less overwhelmed, allowing you to stay in the game for the long term.

Finding a Support Network: The Importance of Building a Community of Like-Minded People for Accountability and Inspiration

No one changes the world alone. Behind every successful movement, every sustained effort, and every impactful initiative, there's a network of people who provide support, encouragement, and accountability. Finding a community of like-minded individuals can be the key to staying inspired and preventing burnout.

1. The Power of Collective Energy

When you surround yourself with people who share your passion and commitment, their energy can lift you up when yours is running low. The collective energy of a group provides motivation, encouragement, and a sense of shared purpose that can carry you through difficult times.

Take the story of Leah, a social worker who was passionate about advocating for homeless individuals in her city. The work was emotionally taxing, and there were days when Leah questioned whether she had the strength to continue. But she wasn't alone. Leah was part of a group of fellow advocates and social workers who met regularly to discuss their challenges, share ideas, and offer support. On the days when Leah felt like giving up, her community reminded her of the importance of her work and offered the emotional support she needed to keep going.

The power of collective energy is real. When you're feeling burnt out or discouraged, leaning on your community can reignite your passion and give you the strength to continue. Whether it's a formal group, an online community, or a network of friends, having people around you who share your values can make all the difference.

2. Finding Accountability Partners

Having an accountability partner—someone who shares your goals and checks in with you regularly—can help you stay on track when you're feeling overwhelmed or uninspired. Accountability partners provide a sense of responsibility and motivation, helping you push through the moments when you might otherwise lose momentum.

Consider the story of Ethan and Priya, two friends who were passionate about reducing their carbon footprint. Both had set personal goals to live more sustainably—Ethan wanted to cut down on single-use plastics, while Priya was working to reduce her energy consumption. They decided to become accountability partners, checking in with each other every week to share their progress, celebrate wins, and discuss challenges. This simple act of accountability helped both Ethan and Priya stay committed to their goals, even when life got busy or motivation waned.

Accountability partners don't have to be formal. It could be a friend, a colleague, or someone in your community who shares your passion for a cause. By keeping each other accountable, you'll both be more likely to stay focused and inspired.

3. Learning from Others' Experiences

One of the most valuable aspects of building a support network is the opportunity to learn from others' experiences. No matter how passionate or knowledgeable you are, there's always more to learn from those who have walked the path before you or who are working on different aspects of the same issue.

Take the story of Daniel, a young entrepreneur who wanted to start a social enterprise focused on providing clean water to underserved communities. At first, Daniel felt overwhelmed by the logistics of starting a business, fundraising, and navigating the nonprofit sector. But then he connected with a group of social entrepreneurs who had experience in launching similar ventures. Through their mentorship and advice, Daniel gained the insights and knowledge he needed to overcome obstacles and grow his enterprise.

By surrounding yourself with people who have different perspectives and experiences, you'll gain new ideas, strategies, and solutions to the challenges you face. Your support network can become a well of inspiration and knowledge, helping you stay innovative and energized.

4. Celebrating Wins Together

Celebrating victories—both big and small—is an essential part of sustaining your impact. But celebrating alone can sometimes feel anticlimactic. When you have a support network, you can share your wins with people who understand the effort behind them, making the celebration even more meaningful.

Consider the story of Hannah, a community organizer who worked on a voter registration campaign in her city. After months of hard work, Hannah's team registered thousands of new voters —an incredible success. But what made the victory even sweeter was celebrating it with her team. Together, they reflected on the challenges they had overcome, the late nights and early mornings, and the sense of accomplishment they felt in achieving their goal. That shared celebration deepened their connection and gave them the motivation to keep going.

Celebrating wins with others creates a sense of camaraderie and shared purpose. It reminds you that you're not alone in your efforts and that every victory, no matter how small, is worth acknowledging. By building a community around you, you'll have people to celebrate with, lifting you up and fueling your passion for the next challenge.

Sustaining Your Impact for the Long Term

Staying inspired and preventing burnout in your philanthropic or activist work is a long-term game. It requires self-awareness, intentional rest, and a support network that lifts you up when the work gets tough. By focusing on small wins, reconnecting with your purpose, taking care of yourself, and surrounding yourself with like-minded people, you can sustain your impact for the long haul.

Remember that real change takes time. There will be moments of frustration, exhaustion, and doubt, but those moments are part of the journey. What matters is that you keep going, fueled by your passion and supported by your community.

By staying inspired and preventing burnout, you ensure that your efforts continue to make a difference—both in the lives of those you're helping and in your own. And when the road gets tough, remember this: you're not alone. There are others walking this path with you, cheering you on, and working by your side to create a better world. Together, you can sustain your impact and leave a legacy of lasting change.

CHAPTER 13:
LEAVING A LEGACY

When we think about leaving a legacy, our minds often jump to monumental acts—something huge that forever changes the world. But legacies aren't built in a day, nor are they the result of one grand gesture. Instead, they're the accumulation of small, sustained actions over time. Whether you're passionate about protecting the environment, championing social justice, or improving education, the legacy you leave is the result of consistent effort, dedication, and the impact you have on others.

Leaving a legacy is not just about the tangible changes you create but also about inspiring those who come after you. When we take the long view, we realize that the real power of our actions lies not just in what we do ourselves, but in how we influence others to continue the work long after we're gone. This chapter is about understanding the power of consistency in creating lasting change and inspiring future generations to carry that torch forward.

The Power of Consistency: How Sustained Small Actions Over Time Create Long-Lasting Change

When you look at any significant movement or accomplishment in history, you'll notice a common thread: persistence. Change doesn't happen overnight, and it rarely happens because of one single action. It's the result of sustained effort over time, the kind of consistency that, while it may feel slow in the moment, leads to real, lasting transformation.

1. The Ripple Effect of Small, Consistent Actions

Consider the story of Jadav Payeng, a man from India who has been called the "Forest Man of India." In 1979, after witnessing the devastating effects of deforestation on his native land, Jadav started planting trees. One tree at a time. Every day. He didn't have a grand master plan—just a commitment to restoring the land around him. Decades later, Jadav's daily planting efforts have resulted in the creation of a 1,360-acre forest, home to hundreds of species of wildlife, including elephants, tigers, and deer. His forest is larger than New York's Central Park, and it all started with a single tree.

Jadav's story is a powerful reminder that small, consistent actions, when compounded over time, create immense impact. It's easy to feel like the little things we do won't matter in the long run, but the truth is, they're what matter most. When we take action, even in small ways, we set off a ripple effect that extends far beyond what we can see in the moment.

Think about it: If you decide to dedicate just one hour a week to mentoring a student, or pick up litter at your local park every month, or donate a small portion of your paycheck to a cause you care about, those actions add up. They create change not only in the immediate sense but also inspire others to follow your lead. The key to leaving a legacy isn't in making massive leaps but in committing to consistent steps that move you forward.

2. The Compound Effect of Persistence

This idea of small actions compounding over time is also beautifully illustrated in the work of Wangari Maathai, the first African woman to win the Nobel Peace Prize. Wangari founded the Green Belt Movement in Kenya, an environmental and women's empowerment organization focused on tree planting, environmental conservation, and advocating for women's rights. Like Jadav, Wangari's efforts began with a simple idea: plant trees to combat deforestation and environmental degradation. But she didn't stop there. Wangari understood that real change would come through consistent effort, through educating others, and through mobilizing communities.

Over the course of several decades, Wangari and the women in her movement planted more than 51 million trees across Kenya. These trees helped restore ecosystems, improve local economies, and empower women to take an active role in their communities. Wangari's work didn't happen in a flash—it was the result of years and years of persistence, one tree at a time, one village at a time. And today, her legacy lives on through the Green Belt Movement, which continues to plant trees, advocate for sustainability, and fight for human rights.

Wangari's story teaches us that when we commit to something over the long haul, our actions don't just add up—they multiply. Her life's work is a testament to the idea that even in the face of great challenges, persistence creates progress, and progress leaves a legacy.

3. Applying the Power of Consistency to Your Own Life

Now, you might be thinking, "That's great for Jadav and Wangari, but I don't have decades to dedicate to planting trees or starting a global movement." The good news is, you don't have to. The power of consistency can apply to any cause, in any context. It's not about how much time you have—it's about what you do with the time you're given.

Let's take the example of Kate, a high school teacher who is passionate about improving literacy rates in her community. Kate realized that many of her students weren't reading outside of class because they didn't have access to books at home. Rather than trying to solve the entire literacy problem overnight, Kate started small. Every month, she organized a book drive and invited friends, family, and colleagues to donate gently used books. Over time, Kate built a small library in her classroom and created a lending program for her students. It wasn't a massive initiative, but over the years, the impact on her students was profound. Many students reported that the availability of books at home helped them fall in love with reading and improve their academic performance.

Kate's story shows that consistent, small actions—whether it's hosting a monthly book drive, volunteering a few hours each week, or donating to a cause—can lead to meaningful change over time. The key is to stay committed, even when the progress feels slow. Because those small, sustained efforts will compound into something much bigger than you ever imagined.

Inspiring Future Generations: Teaching Children, Students, or Peers the Value of Giving Back and Creating a Ripple Effect of Impact

As we think about leaving a legacy, it's important to recognize that the most enduring legacies are the ones we pass on to others. When we inspire future generations to carry on the work we've started, we create a ripple effect of impact that extends far beyond our own lifetime. Whether you're a parent, teacher, mentor, or community leader, one of the most powerful things you can do is teach others the value of giving back and inspire them to become changemakers themselves.

1. Lead by Example

One of the most effective ways to inspire others, especially children and young people, is by leading by example. When they see you actively engaged in philanthropy, advocacy, or volunteering, it sends a powerful message that giving back is not just something you talk about—it's something you do.

Take the story of Carlos, a father of three who was deeply committed to environmental conservation. Every Saturday, Carlos and his kids would spend the morning cleaning up a local beach, picking up trash, and sorting recyclables. At first, his children weren't particularly excited about spending their weekends doing this, but over time, they began to take pride in their efforts. They started noticing the difference they were making—how the beach looked cleaner, how wildlife seemed to be thriving more, and how passersby would stop to thank them for their work. Eventually, Carlos's kids began organizing their own clean-up days with friends from school, creating a ripple effect of impact in their community.

Carlos didn't have to give a lecture about the importance of environmental stewardship—he simply showed his children through his own actions. By leading by example, you can inspire those around you to get involved, to care, and to take action.

2. Make Giving a Part of Everyday Life

One of the most powerful ways to instill the value of giving back is by making it a part of everyday life. When philanthropy or volunteering becomes a regular, integrated part of your routine, it normalizes the idea that giving back isn't something special or extraordinary—it's just what we do.

Take the example of Melissa, a single mother who wanted to teach her children about empathy and generosity. Instead of waiting for big charity events or volunteer opportunities, Melissa made giving a part of her family's daily life. Every evening at dinner, she and her kids would talk about one small act of kindness they had done that day—whether it was helping a classmate, sharing a snack, or simply holding the door open for someone. These conversations helped Melissa's children understand that giving back doesn't always have to be a grand gesture—it can be woven into the fabric of everyday life.

As a result, her kids grew up seeing kindness and giving as a natural part of who they were. They volunteered at food banks, organized toy drives during the holidays, and even started their own fundraiser at school for a local animal shelter. By making giving a part of their everyday routine, Melissa created a ripple effect that would extend far beyond her own actions.

3. Create Opportunities for Others to Get Involved

Inspiring future generations to give back often means creating opportunities for them to do so. Whether you're a teacher creating service-learning projects for students, a manager encouraging your employees to participate in volunteer days, or a community member organizing events for your neighborhood, providing opportunities for people to get involved is one of the most powerful ways to spread the impact of your work.

Take the story of Jerome, a college student who started a mentorship program for at-risk youth. Jerome had grown up in a low-income neighborhood and knew firsthand the challenges that many young people faced. He wanted to give back by providing mentorship, but he realized that he couldn't do it alone. So, Jerome reached out to his peers and organized a team of student mentors who committed to working with local middle school students. Over time, the mentorship program grew, and what started as a small initiative led by one student became a campus-wide movement.

Jerome's mentorship program didn't just help the students who were being mentored—it also gave his peers the opportunity to get involved and make a difference. By creating opportunities for others to participate, Jerome amplified the impact of his work and created a legacy that would continue long after he graduated.

4. The Ripple Effect: Your Legacy Lives On Through Others

When you inspire others to get involved—whether it's your children, your students, your colleagues, or your friends—you create a ripple effect that extends far beyond what you can do on your own. Your legacy is no longer just about the actions you've taken, but about the actions you've inspired others to take. And those actions will continue to grow, multiply, and evolve, long after you're no longer directly involved.

Consider the story of Fred Rogers, better known as Mister Rogers, who spent his life teaching children the values of kindness, empathy, and understanding through his television show. While Fred Rogers is no longer with us, his legacy lives on through the millions of people he inspired—both children and adults—who continue to practice and spread the values he taught. The ripple effect of his work has touched generations, and it continues to influence how people approach kindness and community building.

You don't have to be a famous figure like Mister Rogers to leave a similar legacy. Every time you inspire someone else to take action, you're creating a ripple effect that extends far beyond your own efforts. Whether it's teaching a child the value of kindness, mentoring a colleague in their advocacy efforts, or simply leading by example, you're planting seeds that will grow into something much bigger than yourself.

Building a Legacy of Lasting Impact

Leaving a legacy isn't about fame or recognition. It's about making a meaningful, lasting impact—whether through the small, consistent actions you take or the people you inspire along the way. The power of consistency lies in its ability to create real, tangible change over time. And the ripple effect of your efforts extends far beyond what you can see in the present moment.

As you continue your journey in philanthropy, activism, or community building, remember that your legacy is already in the making. Every action you take, every person you inspire, every small win you celebrate contributes to the long-term impact you'll leave behind.

The greatest legacies aren't built on grand gestures—they're built on a lifetime of commitment, persistence, and the ripple effect of inspiring others to do the same. And that is how you leave a legacy that lasts, far beyond your own lifetime.

Conclusion: Your Time to Make a Difference Is Now

You've made it this far, and by now, you're likely feeling the weight of the possibilities that lie before you. The causes that need attention, the communities that need support, and the changes that seem too big to tackle alone—they can feel overwhelming. But here's the truth: *you are more powerful than you think.* Even the smallest actions, when taken with purpose and consistency, can create ripples of change that extend far beyond what you might imagine.

You Are More Powerful Than You Think

It's easy to underestimate your ability to make a difference. Maybe you've asked yourself, "What can one person really do?" or, "How much impact can I have with the limited time, money, or skills I have?" These questions are natural, but the answer is clear: *one person can do a lot.* Change starts with individuals—people who decide to take that first step, however small, and keep moving forward.

Think about the stories we've shared in these chapters: people like Jadav Payeng, who planted a forest one tree at a time; or Wangari Maathai, whose simple act of planting trees became a movement that empowered thousands of women. They didn't wait for permission, expertise, or the perfect opportunity. They started with what they had, and their actions inspired countless others to join them.

Your small actions—whether it's helping a neighbor, donating to a cause, volunteering your skills, or simply raising awareness —*matter.* They set off ripples that can turn into waves, influencing others to act, creating change in your community, and contributing to a larger movement. You don't need to solve every problem to make an impact; you just need to take the first step. And remember, *your effort is enough.*

Start Today, With What You Have

There's a common misconception that we need to wait for the right moment, the perfect time when we have more money, more resources, or more knowledge before we start giving back. But here's the thing: the perfect time rarely, if ever, arrives. The truth is, *there's no need to wait.*

Start today, with the skills, time, and resources you already possess. It doesn't have to be big or grand. Maybe it's as simple as committing to volunteer a few hours a month, using your professional expertise to support a local nonprofit, or mentoring a young person who needs guidance. Maybe it's just about becoming more intentional in your daily choices—like buying from ethical brands, reducing waste, or speaking up for causes you care about.

Take the story of Clara, who started small by organizing a neighborhood clean-up on the weekends. She didn't have a grand plan or a large group of volunteers—just a desire to make her local park cleaner. Over time, her efforts caught the attention of others, and soon, her clean-up turned into a monthly event that brought together people from all over the city. Clara didn't wait for the perfect time or the perfect resources. She started with what she had, and the impact grew from there.

You don't need to have everything figured out to begin. The world needs people who are willing to take that first step, even when the path ahead isn't entirely clear. Start where you are, with what you have, and trust that as you move forward, opportunities will unfold, and your impact will grow.

One Person, One Cause, Endless Possibilities

If there's one message I hope you take away from this book, it's this: *the world needs you.* Not just the well-known activists, not just the people with millions of dollars to donate or massive platforms to speak from—the world needs *each of us* to take part. We are all part of the solution. Whether you're focused on environmental sustainability, social justice, humanitarian aid, or education, there is a place for your voice, your energy, and your unique contribution.

One person, one cause—when you commit to it, *the possibilities are endless*. The world changes because ordinary people choose to act. They see a problem, and instead of turning away or waiting for someone else to fix it, they step in. They make a difference, not because they're extraordinary, but because they *choose* to make a difference. And when enough people make that choice, the collective impact is profound.

So, what will your legacy be? What cause will you choose to stand behind? What actions—big or small—will you take to leave the world a little better than you found it? Whatever you decide, know that your contribution matters. The impact of your efforts may start small, but it can inspire others to join you. Together, we can build a world that is more just, more compassionate, and more sustainable.

The World Is Waiting for You

Now is your time to make a difference. Don't wait for permission, perfection, or the "right" time. The time is now, and the world is waiting for you to step forward. Your actions, your energy, and your passion are needed more than ever.

You are more powerful than you think. Start today, with what you have. And remember: one person, one cause, endless possibilities.

Together, we can change the world.

Resources for Getting Involved

If you're ready to take action and start making a difference, the first step is finding the right opportunities, organizations, and platforms to get involved. Below is a curated list of resources, including volunteer networks, activist platforms, and tools that can help you get started on your journey to making an impact. Whether you're looking for in-person volunteering, online activism, or ways to integrate giving into your daily life, these resources will provide you with a starting point.

Volunteer Opportunities

1. **VolunteerMatch**
   Website: www.volunteermatch.org
   Description: One of the largest online platforms connecting volunteers with nonprofit organizations. You can search for opportunities by location, cause, or skill set, and filter for both in-person and virtual volunteer options.

2. **Idealist**
   Website: www.idealist.org
   Description: Idealist is a global platform that connects individuals with job, internship, and volunteer opportunities in the nonprofit sector. Their extensive search tool helps match people with organizations based on shared values and goals.

3. **All For Good**
   Website: www.allforgood.org
   Description: All For Good is a service of Points of Light, offering a database of volunteer opportunities ranging from environmental conservation to disaster relief. It allows users to browse and sign up for local or virtual volunteer events.

4. **Catchafire**
   Website: www.catchafire.org
   Description: Catchafire connects skilled professionals with nonprofits needing assistance. Whether you're a designer, marketer, or project manager, you can offer your expertise to organizations in need.

ACTIVISM RESOURCES

1. **Change.org**
   Website: www.change.org
   Description: Change.org is a popular platform for starting and signing petitions on a wide range of social and environmental issues. It allows anyone to create a petition, gather support, and mobilize action.

2. **350.org**
   Website: www.350.org
   Description: A global organization dedicated to addressing the climate crisis, 350.org provides resources for climate activism, including ways to join local campaigns, organize events, and participate in digital advocacy efforts.

3. **MoveOn**
   Website: www.moveon.org
   Description: MoveOn focuses on progressive advocacy and activism, offering opportunities to participate in grassroots movements for social justice, democracy reform, and environmental sustainability.

4. **Avaaz**
   Website: www.avaaz.org
   Description: Avaaz is a global activist network that empowers individuals to take action on issues like climate change, human rights, and political corruption. The platform allows you to participate in international campaigns and petitions.

Donation and Charitable Giving Platforms

1. **Kiva**
   Website: www.kiva.org
   Description: Kiva is a micro-lending platform that allows individuals to make small loans to entrepreneurs around the world. Your loan helps people in developing countries start businesses and improve their lives, and you get repaid over time.

2. **GlobalGiving**
   Website: www.globalgiving.org
   Description: GlobalGiving connects donors with grassroots nonprofit projects worldwide. You can search for causes you care about and donate directly to projects focused on disaster relief, education, healthcare, and more.

3. **GoFundMe**
   Website: www.gofundme.com
   Description: GoFundMe is a crowdfunding platform where individuals and organizations can raise funds for charitable causes, community projects, medical expenses, and more.

Online Learning and Educational Resources

1. **TED Talks**
   Website: www.ted.com
   Description: TED Talks offers a vast library of inspirational and educational talks from experts on a wide range of topics, including philanthropy, social justice, environmental sustainability, and more.

2. **Coursera**
   Website: www.coursera.org
   Description: Coursera partners with universities and organizations worldwide to offer free and paid courses on topics like social entrepreneurship, climate change,

public health, and nonprofit leadership.

3. **edX**

Website: www.edx.org

Description: edX offers free courses from top universities and organizations in areas like humanitarian work, environmental science, and social impact, helping individuals develop the skills needed to contribute to global causes.

Tools for Digital Activism

1. **Thunderclap**

Website: www.thunderclap.it

Description: A tool that allows activists to amplify their message on social media. Thunderclap lets people schedule a message that will be broadcast simultaneously across multiple social media accounts, creating a viral effect.

2. **Action Network**

Website: www.actionnetwork.org

Description: Action Network provides tools for organizing, mobilizing, and managing online activism campaigns. It's perfect for creating petitions, sending mass emails, and coordinating grassroots movements.

Action Plan Template

Getting involved in philanthropy or activism can be overwhelming, but breaking it down into an actionable plan makes it more manageable. This template will help you define your cause, set clear goals, and outline the steps you'll take to make a difference.

Step 1: Define Your Cause

What is the main cause or issue you want to focus on? Think about what moves you, what makes you feel passionate, or what problem you want to help solve.

Example:
Cause: *Environmental sustainability—specifically reducing plastic waste in my community.*

Step 2: Identify Your Strengths and Resources

What skills, talents, or resources do you have that can help you contribute to this cause? Consider your professional skills, network, free time, or creative talents.

Example:
Strengths/Resources: *I have graphic design skills, a network of local business owners, and a few hours of free time on weekends.*

Step 3: Set SMART Goals

SMART goals are specific, measurable, achievable, relevant, and time-bound. Break down your big idea into smaller, actionable goals that you can track over time.

Example:
Goal 1: *Organize two community workshops in the next three months*

to educate residents about reducing plastic waste.
Goal 2: *Partner with three local businesses to implement a plastic-free initiative by the end of the year.*

Step 4: Outline Action Steps

What specific actions will you take to achieve your goals? Write down the steps that will move you closer to making an impact.

Example:
Action Steps:

1. *Research local environmental groups and invite guest speakers for the workshops.*
2. *Create flyers and promotional materials for the workshops.*
3. *Reach out to local businesses to discuss how they can reduce plastic waste.*
4. *Schedule regular check-ins with businesses to track progress on the plastic-free initiative.*

Step 5: Build Accountability and Support

Who can support you in your efforts? Accountability partners, mentors, or a support network can help you stay on track and provide encouragement along the way.

Example:
Accountability Partner: *My friend Sarah, who is also passionate about environmental issues, will check in with me monthly to discuss progress and challenges.*

Step 6: Celebrate Wins and Reflect

What milestones will you celebrate along the way? Take time to reflect on your progress, celebrate small victories, and make adjustments if needed.

Example:
Milestones to Celebrate:
Successfully hosting the first community workshop.
Securing partnerships with three local businesses.

Step 7: Adjust and Keep Moving Forward

As you begin taking action, you might need to adjust your goals or strategies. Stay flexible, learn from setbacks, and keep moving forward with your mission.

By using this action plan template, you'll have a clear roadmap for making an impact in your chosen cause. Remember, the key to lasting change is consistency and perseverance. Every small step you take brings you closer to a better world.

Now it's your turn. Start today. Start with what you have. And watch your actions create waves of change.